Journeys Through Life: Tales of Change

How individuals have changed their lives with therapy

Terry J. Martin, LCSW, DCSW

JMT Publications • Shirley, Indiana 47384

Journeys Through Life: Tales of Change
Published by JMT Publications
501 White Street
Shirley, Indiana 47384

Library of Congress Control Number: 2008927525

ISBN: 0970304579
13 digit ISBN: 0-9703045-7-5

Contents

Dedication

I dedicate this book to all of the Soldiers and their Families who I have had the honor of helping and who give selflessly to our country for our freedom.

To my Ohana in Hawaii, who have helped to make this writing project truly inspirational and memorable.

I also thank my loving parents in Heaven who taught me how important Ohana (family) is to all of us.

My Ohana: Mitzi, Lucy, Morris, Gene, and especially Corkie who have always loved and supported me unconditionally in my work and have been with me on my Journey in Life and my own personal Tales of Change.

I thank my brother and sister who helped me to understand what the experience of sibling rivalry really means and the impact it can have in our life.

I also thank God for making Hawaii and allowing me to journey here and work and live in such a beautiful and spiritual place.

Foreword

Clinicians around the world put their skills to practice everyday amid a myriad of client complaints, problems, situations and otherwise unfortunate life events. The primary focus for the clinician is always to empower these folks to learn, grow and heal from their experiences. It is well understood and embraced by Terry J. Martin that this occurs only through a delicate process of providing his clients with a safe, respectful and warm place to work through whatever the presenting problem happens to be. Through my years of engaging and learning from clinicians in both the Department of Defense and civilian communities, I have found that many struggle to inform others of the processes involved in finding that place in therapy where the clinician and client become a team – a team intent upon ridding the client of any unnecessary "baggage", building on existing personal strengths and adding new skills to help the individual navigate life challenges in a more healthy and informed manner.

The author understands this challenge and the human condition well and, therefore, masterfully created a series of client stories of which wonderfully highlight the sometimes arduous to explain processes involved in therapy. This book will expose the professional and client level readers (and everyone in between) to the intricacies and art of the "dance" we call therapy. The author walks the reader through the journey of the change process – a process worth the time, effort and attention of anyone concerned with living fully, intentionally and purposefully.

What excites me most about this book is that many folks who have previously contemplated engaging themselves in therapeutic services are afforded an insider's perspective to the therapeutic process. These readers will find that both their skepticism of therapy and their life situations are normalized and respected. What is more, the author shows the reader that many clients' lives have been forever changed due to their willingness to find the courage to change and accept their responsibility in the self-awareness and self-healing process.

Mr. Martin has been a personal friend and colleague of mine for many years now. In our shared efforts to help military families in crisis, I witnessed his ability to help others identify and articulate personal challenges, as well as subsequently follow this identification with a meaningful therapeutic exchange. His clinical skill level is shared only amongst the most experienced craftsmen and craftswomen of our broad clinician trade. As a steward of the therapy profession, Mr. Martin has helped me and countless others in our own efforts to better able assist others in need by remaining a true, consistent and well-informed colleague and mentor.

If you, the reader, understand the everlasting benefits of the therapeutic process, or are simply interested in learning if it might be useful in your own life, I suggest that this thoughtful depictment of therapy and processes of change is a must read. That said, I recommend this book heartily, for it is a gem of real-life narrative, focused on the core of the condition of being human in our present day global, societal and individual struggles and triumphs. Life is about choice. Choose this book to continue your professional (clinicians) or personal (clients or potential clients) insight and development journey.

Jason L. Durr MSW

Jason L. Durr MSW, formerly a U.S. soldier, behavioral health social worker and medical social worker, is currently a medical social work supervisor at one of the largest and most well respected hospices in the United States. Jason prides himself on developing and nurturing professionals in the helping community charged with empowering individuals and families in need. It is to the author's credit that the interest shown here in his book, Journeys Through Life -Tales of Change, is viewed as playing a large part to that same end. Enjoy the process!

Prologue

The following stories are based on some of my professional and personal experiences. All characters are composites, loosely based on actual cases I have treated, but all characters and events described are fictional. It is my goal to encourage those challenged by emotional issues, or who are in need of emotional support, to seek out professional help in the form of therapy. Hopefully, these stories will provide additional knowledge and insight into many of the emotional challenges people sometimes encounter in their lives.

I, taking on the character of Doc, take you on these journeys of choice with each of these fictional characters. Like Doc, I am a licensed and clinically trained cognitive behavioral therapist who has over 20 years of experience helping clients develop insight into their lives through therapy. This insight can help them during their own personal life journey if they so choose. Doc paints a landscape full of intrigue and challenges for each of these characters. He helps them identify self-sabotaging and irrational behaviors as well as where their self-defeating tendencies originate.

Doc uses Rational Emotive Therapy as a treatment modality to help Susan, Walker and John understand and learn to accept that some of their negative behaviors were probably learned during their childhood; some from environmental factors and social learning, but to a large degree each of them have strong inborn biological tendencies to upset themselves. Doc helps to educate these clients away from a life of self-destruction by helping them to identify these irrational and self-defeating beliefs that are rigid, extreme, unrealistic, and illogical. Through active facilitation, he encourages them to forcefully and actively dispute the irrational beliefs and replace them with more rational and self-helping ones.

By attaining a more rational and self-constructive philosophy of themself, others and the world, each of these characters can behave and express emotions in a more life-serving manner, and function within their individual story in many other positive, adaptive ways. Doc utilizes his brush on the canvas with finesse and adds even deeper textures and hues as each characters story unfolds. He illustrates that through combined cognitive, emotive, and behavioral – awareness a client can develop insight, as well as a quite persistent and forceful, attack on a client's serious emotional problems that can possibly ameliorate or remove them - and keep them removed.

Walker, an unemployed health care executive from the Midwest who worked for a residential care facility that housed geriatric–psychiatric patients. Walker was an up and coming executive, talented and gifted in the area of mental health care facility management, who was in his early 30s and employed by a leading corporation in the field for six months. He knew that things within the corporation weren't as they should be after working there for one month. Nurses changed reports after they had been submitted for his review and approval, and patients abusing other patients was not reported either to him or the proper authorities. Doc helps Walker to identify the abusive and unethical behaviors that have been perpetrated on Walker by his narcissistic and toxic boss, and assists a reluctant Walker to empower himself to make the right choices by following through with a cooperative effort with a Senator interested in investigating the incident.

Walker's empowerment and subsequent actions would bring attention on a national basis that would lead to investigation of the corporation's illegal and unethical activities. Walker's actions and their results helped him to move toward freedom from his self-imposed prison of victimhood.

John was a recovering alcoholic in his late thirties who grew up in a working class blue collar Irish family in which he was abused both physically and verbally as a child by his emotionally detached father. John struggles with intimacy daily in his life.

John's history is fraught with homelessness, alcoholism, violence, and abandonment. John came to see Doc and never missed an appointment though he always questioned why he needed to come and work on himself. Doc ultimately helped John begin to navigate the maze of his emotionally detached life.

Susan, whose life is out of control, comes to therapy in a state of panic. She sees her seven-year, verbally and emotionally abusive marriage possibly coming to an end and she is frightened of being alone. Doc is challenged with helping Susan as she is resistant to make healthy choices to help change her current situation that may help lessen her anxiety. Though Susan participates in several months of therapy, Doc is unable to convince Susan to continue in therapy and do the work she must do to effect a change in her life. She is reluctant to share her innermost thoughts even with her therapist, and resists all changes proposed that threaten the "caretaker" role she performs with aplomb. Susan chooses to stay stuck in her dysfunctional marriage and absolutely refuses to relinquish her caretaker role in her marriage.

To all who are entering psychotherapy: you are about to embark on an exciting, challenging, rewarding and ultimately life changing experience. I wish you the best of luck, and, most of all, the courage to go the distance in the pursuit of the inner wholeness which lies at the end of your journey.

Please join Doc as he shares his journals and takes you on a very intimate and personal journey with Susan, Walker, and John.

Doc Hits The Road

It was 1998 and just another typical hot day in late August in the Midwest. The temperature was 95 degrees, the humidity hit 100 %, and there was no chance of rain in the five day forecast. Walking outside, Doc's clothes were damp in seconds and he felt like an oven had been opened in his face. It was stifling and unbearable and all Doc wanted to do was to stay indoors under the air conditioning. Some people weren't lucky enough to have air conditioning in their homes. It was still considered a luxury to many people, and many of the old apartment buildings did not have central air. If you were lucky, you might rent one with a window unit and pray it didn't go out on a day like today. Midwestern people spend a lot of time talking to each other about the weather as it is always changing daily. Doc found himself often doing this. The midwestern United States is the only place in which it can be 75 degrees on Christmas Eve and below zero on Christmas Day.

Doc had lived in the Midwest for most of his life and was becoming bored and looking for an adventure and a big change of scene. He knew he probably had to move out of his comfort zone if he was to experience something challenging, different and exciting. Doc was ready to move on and the decision to do so was easy to make that day, after the air conditioner broke and Doc's house became like an oven.

"I have to move to greener and most definitely cooler pastures," Doc opined.

Doc couldn't believe how quickly the summer had come and gone. It was already Monday, August 24th, and Labor Day was nearing. Doc closed the door and rushed out over the threshold, almost tripping. A package was leaning against the outside screen door; it said it was an overnight package on the outside. Doc looked at the return address and saw that is was sent by Mr. Setton in San Francisco. Doc was running late and didn't have time to open it. He would look at the contents later.

Doc's hair was still wet and he didn't have time to dry it. It wouldn't matter if he had dried his hair; in this humidity it would just get wet again. The humidity felt heavy in the air, and smoke spewing from the stacks of busy factories made the sky look even more gray and ominous. The intensity of the sun made staying outside longer than five minutes unbearable.To stay outside longer than five minutes, a person needed to wear a hat or carry an umbrella for protection.

The risk of getting sun stroke or sunburned was a constant hazard to many people especially those as fair as Doc. Doc's northern European ancestry blessed him with light blond hair, hazel eyes and a fair complexion ensured that the sun would always find him. Doc discovered that there wasn't a sun screen that could protect his skin from burning. He had used sunscreens with a 60 rating and still got sunburned.

As Doc got into his car and turned the key he immediately turned the air conditioner on. The car felt like the inside of a pizza oven, and the temperature had to be at least 130 degrees Fahrenheit inside. Doc was wearing a blue linen suit, white shirt, red tie and new black wing-tip shoes that were killing his feet. He parked his car with seven minutes to spare before his 9:00 a.m. interview for the Clinical Director position with a halfway house. Doc looked at the package on the seat that Mr.Setton had sent.

"I wonder if it is a job offer?" He was running late and didn't have time to open it. Doc silently told himself, "I'll look at the contents after I finish this interview."

Doc couldn't wait!

"I have five minutes and am too excited and have to see everything that was inside now."

Doc's fingers fumbled as he tried to find the drawstring to open the package. Finally, as he looked inside, he saw what looked like a contract and a letter of employment. He pulled out the contents and briefly looked at them. It was 8:57 a.m.; Doc had to get going if he was going to be on time for the interview. Coming in late wouldn't make a good impression.

Doc was so excited, he couldn't quit wondering about what the contract said. All Doc had time to do was briefly scan the letter offering him a job. It would have to wait until he finished the interview and was able to finish reading everything in the envelope.

"I must refocus my attention on this job interview or the employer would surely pick up on my disconnect and my excitement," Doc thought. He knew never to present himself in an interview this way, as it could possibly alienate a prospective employer especially when the job you are applying for is a clinical position.

Excitedly, Doc walked up the seven steep steps that led to two beautifully handcrafted mahogany wood doors decorated with beautiful etched leaded glass and carved brass knobs shaped like a lion's head that opened onto the reception area of Hills Halfway House. Doc was astounded and blinded briefly by a sea of men in orange jumpsuits. The men huddled close to each other on the front lawn and a thick cloud of cigarette smoke wafted toward Doc. He dodged the smoke, fearing that he would go into the interview smelling of cigarettes and this, similar to being late, never makes a good impression during an interview. As tight as the job market had been recently, Doc believed he needed every advantage he could get, and being late and smelling wasn't that edge.

Clutching the brass railing carefully, Doc reached the top. He could finally see, and the intense blinding glare was gone momentarily from his vista. Doc was able to refocus his eyes.

"I knew I should have brought my sunglasses from the car," Doc thought.

He opened the glass doors and noticed the hallway was an incredibly polished, white travertine marble floor that was so clear that he could see his reflection.

"I wonder who does the cleaning of these beautiful floors," Doc wondered.

Doc turned the corner and almost tripped over a big buffer that was noisily polishing the floor and quickly had the answer to his pondering. A man in an orange jumpsuit was at the controls and Doc was sure that it must be one of the residents. He wondered if this might not be part of a vocational treatment plan that would allow him to gain marketable skills and find employment once he was released from the halfway house.

Doc found the Executive Director's office. His hand froze on the door handle.

He kept asking himself the question over and over in his head: "What is my relationship with this?"

Doc had an epiphany.

The relationship became apparent quickly, and Doc knew this was not where he wanted to work or live anymore. He did not want to make it his future and knew that if he stayed put it would surely become an obstacle, impeding Doc's ability to move forward in his life. Doc felt a profound stirring in his heart that there was something even better waiting for him. An opportunity of a lifetime literally dropped at his feet just a couple of hours ago, and Doc needed to accept this offer. Doc wasn't going to waste the Executive Director's time at the halfway house or his own time. He wasn't interested in this position or in staying in the midwest, and he already had a great job offer.

Doc took his sweaty hand off of the office door and quickly walked back down the polished hallway toward the etched, leaded glass doors. He braced his eyes for the sun's glare and carefully walked back down the stairs and through the blinding sea of orange.

Skipping back to the car, Doc realized he had just made an important choice that would greatly change his life. He was excited and also a little frightened. Doc had lived in the midwest all of his forty-some years, and the region was part of his own personal comfort zone. Doc kept repeating to himself over and over, "I wonder what San Francisco looks like? What is the weather there like? What are the people like?" These questions would all be answered in time.

Doc opened his car door and got in quickly. He dialed his cell phone and called the executive director. She was expecting him in her office within the next minute, and even though it was short notice, Doc felt it was better to cancel than waste her time interviewing for a job he probably wouldn't accept if offered, knowing he had a dream come true to live and work in the City by the Bay. Doc had wanted to go there since he was sixteen, as he was intrigued by the many things available there to explore and experience.

Doc's mental images ranged from cable cars to Golden Gate Park to Alacatraz.

"Mrs. Bryson, I am sorry to have to cancel at the last minute our interview but I received a great career opportunity out of state this morning."

"Would you reconsider the offer if I matched what they were offering after we meet?"

"Mrs. Bryson it's not about the money. It is about the opportunity to work and live in San Francisco, a dream I have had for a long time in my life. I have decided to seize this opportunity and begin a new journey in my life."

After some pleasantries she wished Doc the best. The choice he made that day changed Doc's life over the past ten years in so many positive and profound ways. Doc never looked back or regretted his decision. He never imagined that he would consider moving again even further from the midwest and his roots for another great opportunity. This story will come later.

Doc started the car and placed a heavy foot on the accelerator. He wanted to get home as fast as possible. Turning onto Grand Boulevard, Doc knew he was only two blocks away from his house. Excitedly pulling into the driveway, Doc almost hit the lawnmower he had left there. Whistling, he turned the key to his duplex and saw Mitzi. She was Doc's beautiful red chow chow and she was wagging her tail, with the incredible smile creasing her face that Doc came to expect every time he came home. Mitzi never lets Doc set his briefcase down until she sniffs it, as well as Doc. After Mitzi's inspection, Doc gave her a good petting and fed her a treat. Mitzi was pleasantly spoiled. Lucy, Doc's adorable seal point Persian cat, was lying on the windowsill watching all the birds and didn't even look up. Doc was certain Lucy wished she were outside, chasing the bevy of birds that she spent hours watching while Doc was at work. Doc adored them both and felt blessed to have them in his life.

Doc set his briefcase down on the dining room table and sat down on a chair finally to catch his breath. He didn't know what to do first: He wasn't sure if he wanted to yell, cry, call everyone and tell them of his huge decision and the journey on which he was about to embark or just sit quietly for a few more minutes and enjoy this joyful moment. He was so ecstatic, but also felt a little numb. Doc guessed it was all of that adrenalin that was still pumping through his body from earlier that morning. Doc reminded himself that it had been three hours since he first read the letter and that he should be over it by now, but he wasn't.

After recovering his breath and feeling a little more relaxed, Doc began to scan each room from floor to ceiling and did a mental inventory of what to take with him and what to leave. He suddenly became alarmed and thought, "Oh no, I need to get some boxes. I have to call the real estate agent, call a mover, and tell the family ..." The to-do list suddenly seemed endless.

Once the realities of the decision started to sink in, Doc started to have second thoughts.

"Maybe this is too much to take on now in my life." Doc found himself listening to old, negative mental tapes that he thought he had permanently ejected. Some of the messages came bleeding through even after Doc thought he had worked through them.

The negative self-talk continued running through his mind: "Do you think this is worth it? Why don't you just stay here? Everything is comfortable, and you are already settled in your life. Why do you want to leave all of this for the unknown? You will disappoint your family. Why would they support such an extreme decision?"

"STOP!!!!!" Doc yelled. "I won't hear anymore of this negative crap. I am going and God will make it all possible. I want to trust that I am where I need to be at this moment."

Doc kept telling himself over and over, "I have to be in San Francisco in six weeks and get all of my stuff sorted out in that time." The negative self talk continued: "I am 49 years old; am I too old for this adventure? It would take two weeks just to say good-bye to everyone and then I have to face all of the sadness I will feel. Is it worth it?"

"Stop!!!" Doc repeated. He needed to relax and center his mind, hopefully to regain his focus. Meditation was a tool that helped him to get centered quickly, and Doc routinely meditated twice a day for twenty minutes Doc turned the blinds down, unplugged the phone and closed his eyes.

The next thing Doc knew was that noon had arrived already, and he felt a lot calmer and more focused. "I am now ready to sit down and begin to prioritize items and to develop my transition plan," Doc affirmed. Meditation never eliminated his stressors; but it did help him to manage them in a more positive and healthy way, and with clarity.

Doc walked through the house, making a mental note of what he was taking and what was going to be given away or sold. Doc's Mother had passed less than a year before, and his father had passed seven years ago. He still had a lot of their stuff and hadn't gone through any of it.

"I will think about it tomorrow," Doc told himself, and he had started to believe that. Denial works for a while, but then the reality of the issues you are dealing with demand confrontation. Doc decided that some of his Mom and Dad's stuff that he had could be donated to a charity that could really help people who were in need. "I must call them tomorrow," he noted, and wrote this down on the to-do list, which was growing by the hour. Pretty soon it would be unmanageable

It became increasingly more difficult for Doc to let go as time went by, not only of some of his stuff but that of his parents as well. His mom kept every card and gift she ever received, and there were trash bags full of cards from every holiday: Mothers' Day, birthday, Christmas, even Halloween.

Doc went to the Land of Denial (an imaginary place that people go to when they don't' want to deal with the present moment) again and began to convince himself that he could just wait until he got to California to give their things to charity. (Who was he kidding?)

He would have time to go through all of his personal baggage later and sort all of this stuff out in California. Doc told himself over and over, "It will be easier this way." He knew it was foolish to move all of this stuff with him when it was logistically and fiscally not prudent to do so. Doc just wasn't ready to deal with saying goodbye to all of his stuff. He had gotten comfortable hauling it around with him wherever he went. Doc found out that people let go of their stuff and leave the Land of Denial only when they are ready. Doc guessed he wasn't quite ready yet.

He knew he was moving physically, but one question nagged at him. "Am I really running away and taking all of my stuff with me?" Doc believed in his heart and soul that this move was an opportunity to move on. He had become too comfortable over the course of time, dragging his emotional baggage around with him.

Doc struggled internally to overcome any resistance to this move. He knew it would help if he could get into a state of grace. He could get there by being thankful through affirmations, acknowledging the blessings he had in his life. This method had helped Doc in the past to change the paradigm from negative self-talk to positive self-talk. "Thank you God for all of the blessings in my life," Doc intoned.

Doc reflected back on his own family of origin, and became very aware of how change of any kind was viewed by his parents. It was viewed with skepticism and cynicism and always questioned. Doc remembered wanting to share with his mother the experience and excitement he had of going to Paris for the first time and when he finally did, his mother asked, "Why would you want to go there?"

"Why not?" Doc responded. He asked his mother why she never wanted to experience change or to travel to exotic places.

"I don't leave my home or the city I live in. I have everything I need right here," his mother replied.

He understood then that his mom's fear and intense resistance to change kept her from stepping onto another path, and he believed it kept her from really becoming the woman she always wanted to be. He reminded himself often whenever he was facing the same fears how parent's behaviors impact on us as we grow and develop into adulthood. He knew better than to give in to fear. He recognized that in his case, the apple didn't fall too far from the tree. To this day, Doc still finds himself struggling with some of these same fears whenever change is imminent.

Doc's positive self-talk reaffirmed his decision not to become complacent in his life like his mother did, and to view change as a chance for personal growth.

He realized earlier in his 30s that he couldn't be around negative energy for too long, as it sticks like Velcro and becomes entangled in your heart. In order to survive the onslaught that negative thinking people try and pile on, you have to exit the stage right or it can become part of your persona.

People who resist change because of their fear of what might happen give into this all encompassing and insidious negative energy. This can prevent and/or limit an individual from growing intellectually, spiritually, and emotionally in their lives.

Doc had an established clinical practice in the midwest, and he had to act fast to close it down and transfer clients to his colleagues. Doc really wanted to go to California and have a totally new experience. He was elated to see where this career opportunity might possibly lead. His family thought he had lost all of his senses and was taking a huge gamble, and they could not support the move. After much angst, Doc finally made his mind up. "With or without their support I am going and there is no turning back or changing my mind." The apple was going to leave the tree.

A week had gone by but Doc felt like it had only been a couple of days since he received the letter from Mr. Setton. "I haven't done a thing except write up numerous lists and chat with friends on the phone about how excited I am about the upcoming move," Doc realized. "I have to get out of this bed and get this apartment cleaned up before Linda arrives." Sunday was always a day Doc liked just to lie in bed and read the paper, watch a football game and then maybe stop over at his mom's house and see what she was having for dinner. Unfortunately he would not be able to enjoy his typical Sunday. He was going to spend most of the morning with Linda going over real estate comparisons, taking photos of the property and listening to her lecture incessantly on the importance of curb appeal, manicured lawns and how the kitchen had to be immaculate when she had an open house especially if the potential buyer was a woman. "A kitchen sells a woman," Linda would state frequently

He put the last dish in the dishwasher and heard Mitzi barking. Doc looked at his watch and realized it was already 9:00 a.m. Mitzi has incredible hearing and could hear cars drive up the street before they ever got in front of the house. She would then start her barking way before any visitor would be in front of the house. Looking outside, Doc saw Linda parking her car, and when she got out of her car he observed that she was dressed very well. Doc definitely felt underdressed that day, wearing tennis shoes, jeans and a t-shirt. On the other hand, Linda dressed professionally. She was wearing a dark blue suit with a white blouse that had a modest amount of lace on the sleeves and around the neck. Doc also noticed that she carried herself like a runway model as she walked up the driveway. Wearing black patent leather heels that were at least two to three inches in height, she appeared to glide up the slight incline in the drive with very little effort. "I guess you have to be a woman to master that," he mused. Linda had light naturally blond hair that was pulled back in a bun with a gold hair braid. Without a doubt, she was stunning, stately and professional, and she carried herself with confidence.

She came highly recommended by one of Doc's dear friends, Esther, who raved about her success rate selling properties for close to asking price in a short period of time. Esther said, "Doc, Linda can sell anything in a short span of time even in a depressed market. She presents well and has an ability to connect with all kinds of clients and she has a gift to close all sales with a 99 % track record." With that dramatic recommendation from Esther, Doc was confident that she was the one that could sell his house.

Linda was a striking woman and appeared to be in her early 40s, but Doc would never presume to ask her age. He had learned that mistake years ago with a woman he dated. He never heard from her after the third date, when he stumbled into that fateful question. Linda appeared very confident and was decidedly attractive, and somehow Doc believed that she knew she was. Doc wasn't going to attempt to date her; he just wanted her to sell his home and fast.

He opened the front door and before she sat down on the couch, Doc blurted out, "Linda, how much do you think I can get for the house, and how soon do you think we can get it sold?"

"Hold on Doc," Linda said abruptly. "First things first, Doc. I am here to sell your house."

"Linda, please sit down."

"Doc, this is not a good time to sell property. The market is way down. Your house looks like it is in good shape from what I saw on the outside, and that is a positive, and it has good curb appeal. You might have to rent it out a while after you leave and have the renters agree to have it shown. I will have a couple of open houses for you while you are gone."

"Linda, I certainly didn't want to hear that. I have owned this duplex and have dealt with renters for ten years, and I was so looking forward to having my own home and fixing my own water heater when it broke, rather than someone else's."

"Doc, I understand your concerns and feelings as I have been there myself. I can assure you this is probably only going to be for a short period of time. Doc, the real estate market in the Midwest is like the weather. It can change in a flash."

Doc and Linda both chuckled.

"I hear you have a pretty good track record, so I am confident if anyone can do it I am sure you can."

"Thanks for the encouragement. Esther said your house was in great condition and she was right."

"Linda, I guess I don't have a lot of choices in the matter. If I want to get to my new job in six weeks I have to get busy now. If renting the house out temporarily until I get it sold is what I have to do, then so be it. I will put it in God's hands and trust that He will send me the right buyer for my home."

"That's a good attitude to have, Doc, especially with your time line to start work in six weeks. I need to take some photos inside and outside and look at your basement and then finish walking through the rest of your house. I will try to be out of here shortly."

"Oh good," Doc said to himself, "I can get back in bed and read my newspaper and maybe catch a game." He couldn't wait to get back to his comfort zone.

Doc never did get to get back in bed and read or watch a game. Linda finally completed all of the photos and she and Doc needed to agree on a listing price for the house and sign the necessary papers. He looked over at the clock on the stove and noticed it was 6:00 p.m. Nine hours had elapsed since Linda walked through the door.

"Doc, I am done and will call you Tuesday after I finish all of the comparisons in the neighborhood. Then I'll be able to recommend what price to list your house at and put it in the multi listings book."

Doc walked Linda to the door and, yawning, felt physically exhausted from the day's activities. He had had enough of this change activity for one day. It was time to go to bed and collapse.

As he lay in bed, too tired to fall asleep, he knew he had to focus and work on the coordination of the physical move of his household goods. It had been almost two weeks since he had received the offer of employment, and the clock was ticking. Doc only had four weeks to get all of this organized.

"I will deal with that tomorrow. Now I have to get some sleep."

Doc woke up the next morning to the phone ringing and, rubbing his eyes, saw the alarm clock on the nightstand flashing 8:00 o'clock.

"Hello?"

"Doc, this is Linda. I think I have the right price to sell your house. Can I stop by later to show you the comparison in your neighborhood?"

"Linda today isn't a good day. I have a lot of tasks to start organizing if I am going to make my deadline to be out of here. The movers are coming over at noon to give me an estimate. What price did you come up with?"

"How does $149,900 sound?"

"Linda I think the house is worth a little more than that with all of the remodeling I have done over the past year."

"I agree Doc, but this isn't a good market and I am afraid if we price it too high we might turn a lot of potential buyers off and the property might become stale in the market. Doc, the more we can show it the more we can increase the odds of finding the right buyer."

"Linda, I trust your recommendation. List it at $149,900."

It was already 1:30 in the afternoon and there was no sign of the movers. Doc dozed off on the couch and was awakened by Mitzi barking at the front door. Her red tail was wagging incessantly. She was a good watch dog and the best security system a person could get. Doc knew no one was going to get by her unless they were invited and she knew them. Finally the movers had arrived. Looking at his watch, he noticed that it was 3:30 in the afternoon.

He opened the door and a man walked past him and into the house. When he encountered Mitzi, he immediately retreated back to the porch.

"Hello my name is Norman and I am the estimator to look at what you have to move. Are you Doc?"

"Yes, but give me a minute while I put the dog in the back yard." Doc knew that if he didn't put her in the back yard she would follow the movers throughout the house, barking until they left. They were in her territory and she wanted them to know that.

Norman walked through the house and continuously wrote down items that Doc told him he wanted to move.

"I am finished, and we will mail the quote to you in a couple of days." An hour had elapsed since he arrived. He had hurriedly gone through the home and Doc wondered if he got everything written down or if there would be unexpected expenses on the day of the move. Norman never once apologized for being two and half hours late, nor did he bother to say good bye.

"Good bye Norman, and thank you."

"Oh yeah, what was your name again?"

"Doc."

"Oh yeah, I forgot," he mumbled as he walked down the steps.

"Do I want this man moving my personal things?" Doc wondered. "I need to meditate on this decision."

As Doc walked towards the kitchen he heard the phone ringing.

"Doc, hello this is Linda." It had been two weeks, and Linda didn't have one interested buyer yet. She had already done eight open houses. "Doc, be optimistic," she advised.

"Linda, this isn't looking too promising. I leave in two weeks and I have half of my personal belongings packed. I was also packing all of my parents' personal items as well." Doc decided at the last minute to take his parents' stuff with him and sort it all out in California. He just couldn't go through their stuff now. He had too many things going on in his life. He needed some emotional down time to go through the grieving process of letting go of the familiar, and Doc wasn't ready and didn't have the time now to do it.

"Linda, I have decided to put everything in storage. You will just have to show the apartment empty. I will call you before I leave and you already have a set of keys to the house. I've got to go as I have ten more things I have to get done today. Good bye Linda."

Doc was not looking forward to being a renter again, but he couldn't buy property until his house sold. He lucked out, as Mr. Setton referred him to a great rental agent for condos. The agent had obtained Doc a condo on the 12th floor overlooking the San Francisco Bay near the marina that would accept Mitzi and Lucy. They offered Doc a short term, six month lease. Things were starting to fall into place.

The day of departure was finally here and when Doc was putting Mitzi and Lucy in the car, he saw Linda driving up the street. Mitzi immediately recognized her as she was always at the house having open houses or showing it in the evenings. Mitzi had finally accepted her as just another member of the household pack.

Linda ran from her car, suddenly throwing her arms around Doc with tears streaming down her rosy red cheeks and hugging him tightly. Doc noticed that the times Linda came to show the house, she was a little guarded and didn't disclose any personal information. He wondered what her story was. He found her present behavior a little surprising as it was totally unexpected.

"Doc, I will miss you and Mitzi. Please have a safe and blessed journey, and I wish you the best of luck on your journey."

Mitzi surprised both Doc and Linda by kissing her hand and wanting to be petted. Linda had become part of the family. Doc put the last of his items in the car and started the engine. Backing down the driveway, he waved to Linda and noticed Mitzi wagging her tail and sticking her head out of the window in the rear view mirror. Mitzi appeared to feel like she was chasing imaginary rabbits and squirrels.

"Linda, I'll call you when I get settled. You have my cell phone number. Please call me anytime if you get a contract and don't worry about the two-hour time difference."

"You got it, Doc."

On the way out of town, Doc stopped by his dear friend Esther's house. Esther was his spiritual sister, and was his rock most of his life. Hurriedly walking down the stairs to greet him, Esther almost lost her footing when she embraced Doc.

"Doc, I will miss you very much," babbled Esther as tears streamed down her porcelain cheeks.

"Esther, I will miss you as well," Doc replied. "Esther as we have always agreed upon in our relationship as friends, it is not the quantity of time we spend with each other but the quality of that time." Esther has been to visit Doc every year since he moved. She says they talk more now to each other than they did when they lived in the same town. It is the quality not the quantity that ensures the growth of a relationship.

"We have 25 years of unbelievable quality time as friends and I look forward to 25 more years. Doc, I am sad you are leaving, but I am also very happy that you are taking a chance to pursue a dream of yours. I have known for a long time that you needed to move on from this place. Doc, I am so happy for you to be able to go to California and it truly is a blessing."

"Thanks Esther, I can always count on you to lift my spirits. Esther give me a hug. You have my cell phone number. I really have to go if I want to be in Tulsa by nightfall."

Doc waved to Esther as he drove down her driveway towards Bauer Road, the westward path that was going to take him to his new home. Doc was still weeping as he turned onto the interstate on ramp, but he was finally on the highway heading west down Interstate 44. He never looked back, and anticipated being in Tulsa by 6:00 p.m.

Doc repeated to himself, "This is a journey that I chose freely". He affirmed to himself on the long drive to Tulsa that God would bless this journey.

Over the next seven days, Doc was blessed to experience totally new places from Tulsa to Phoenix and new people in this great country of ours. Mitzi and Lucy were content to ride in the back seat with the bed of pillows Doc assembled for them and they never wanted to leave the car. To this day, Doc believes Mitzi could live in the car. One memorable stop Doc made on the trip was to view the magnificent Grand Canyon. As he looked out over this incredible place, he heard his mother's voice repeating the same sentiment that she expressed when Doc went to Paris: "Why would you want to go there?"

Doc's mother liked California but would often say that she felt trapped in her life. Doc believed she was afraid to leave the home she thought offered her the greatest security. Doc's father never seemed to fully embrace his parental or spousal responsibilities with the passion and zeal his mother possessed. He was gone a lot when he was growing up. His mom, on the other hand, was like the Rock of Gibraltar, always solid and there when you needed her. Doc believed his mom was very co-dependent and he saw her assume the roles of caretaker and rescuer often while he was growing up.

Driving cross-country, Doc had many hours in the car to remember and reflect on his life. He reflected on his parents' choices, as they both had struggled with their own personal issues of change. His mom always resisted any and all kinds of change, while his dad always wanted to embrace change at all costs. They were on opposite ends of the risk spectrum.

It was 9:30 p.m. and Doc was an hour outside of Tucson, Arizona. The night sky over the desert was awesome; it seemed as though a person could pluck his own star from the sky. A shooting star suddenly fell from the sky, and Doc was motivated to make a wish. He began to think about how his mom had convinced herself that to maintain control over her life she had to be rigid and resistant to any change. She especially fought the ones his dad was always suggesting to her. Doc's dad was always traveling and wanting to move to go to greener pastures, but his mother saw that as running away from reality. Finally, she dug her heels in and refused to give in to his dad's gypsy whims. This was the only way his mom believed she could provide stability for the family. It was unfortunate that it prevented her from embracing change and looking at the world differently. Doc was aware that all people must choose their own path but recognized that it does help to have healthy people in life who offer support for those on the path. Doc's mother never had a healthy support system, but Doc did.

Doc knew his mom probably saw that wanderlust as being immature and irresponsible. Early on in their marriage, his mom allowed his dad to convince her that the grass was greener across the road or in the next state, but eventually, mom found out it never was.

Doc went to many different schools growing up as the family was always moving. His mom finally got fed up with all of the uncertainty in the family's life. His dad never had a clue as to what all of this upheaval was doing to the family, but Mom did. She kept her heels dug into the ground and never let him drag her up and down the road for a supposedly better opportunity any longer.

"Mom, thanks for standing your ground with Dad," Doc said as he listened to the car radio blare a Patsy Cline song. "It helped me more than you can know. I respect you for standing your ground and understand now why you were afraid of leaving your home, even up to the day you joined Dad in heaven."

"Dad, thanks for your enthusiasm and passion you always showed me when you told me stories of your travels. The stories are always with me as you are now with me on this lonely desert highway going into Tucson and then into Yuma, roads that you traveled often in your life. Thanks Dad for the stories and giving me your desire to travel and seek out new horizons."

"Mitzi and Lucy, I think I found us a place to rest. We will soon be in San Francisco in two days. I am exhausted!" Doc exclaimed as he hit the bed.

When Doc saw the skyline of San Francisco, he got very excited and realized that he had only one month before he started his new job. He could get some sightseeing in. All he had to do now was figure out from the map where to exit off of the highway in bumper to bumper traffic in order to get to Sausalito and his new home.

Doc wondered to himself, "What's with all of this traffic?" as he saw the exit ahead. His excitement continued, and he started to sing along to the song, "California Dreamin'" that was playing on the radio.

Settling In

"Good morning, San Francisco, it's November 21st 1998 in the City by the Bay and it's 7:30 a.m. Expect fog clearing by noon and early morning showers but sunny skies by late afternoon. Traffic on the Golden Gate Bridge is backed up due to an accident and everyone expect 1-2 hour delays in your morning commute"

Doc couldn't believe what the disk jockey had just said on the radio. He was right in the middle of the traffic he was talking about. He had to be downtown at his office on California Street to meet his first client of the day at 9:00 a.m. Doc was still thirty minutes away and it was 7:30 a.m. He didn't know if he was going to make it before 9:00 a.m.

"I have to call my office and tell Maggie to try and reach this client and let him know I would be late."

Maggie was Doc's recently hired receptionist. Doc wondered if Maggie was in the same traffic mess he was in.

"Maggie, this is Doc. I am running late as I am caught in a traffic mess on the Golden Gate Bridge. Can you please call my 9:00 a.m. appointment and tell him that I might be late and offer to reschedule if he wants to? When you get this message please call me on my cell phone."

Doc was glad he had decided to venture out and open his own private practice. The job offer from Mr.Setton at the health center was a good one, and it helped Doc make the decision to move to San Francisco, but he really wanted to have his own private practice again. The independence and autonomy that comes with a private practice was worth the uncertainty that came with it to Doc. Besides it allowed him to have an extra month off before he had to start to work. His office wouldn't be available to move into until the first of November, and who knew when he would be able to take time off again? Doc decided to do some more sightseeing.

Sitting in this traffic nightmare, Doc remembered how Maggie accidentally came into his life. Maggie was a gem; she was married, came from Ireland as a child with her parents and had settled in Chicago. She was in her early 30s, articulate, very striking in appearance and has the brightest carrot red hair Doc had ever seen on anyone. This was combined with a porcelain complexion and sparkling emerald green eyes. She lived in Sausalito in a small house overlooking Alcatraz with her two children. Her husband traveled often for his job and was very supportive of her. Doc also accidentally discovered that they were also neighbors, as she didn't live too far from him.

They met for the first time at a local grocery store on a rainy Sunday close to Halloween in October, at the check out line. She was behind Doc.

"Excuse me sir, but I think you have dropped your driver's license," she said. Looking down on the floor Doc saw she was bending down to pick it up and handed it to him.

"So what kind of Doc are you?" she asked.

"Pardon me?"

"Your license says you are a doctor."

"I am a mental health therapist."

"Pardon me, my name is Maggie Wendt and I hope you don't think I am to forward, but I was wondering if you need any help in your office? I have a lot of experience from when I lived in Chicago and worked in a mental health clinic."

Doc was happy with what he was being told.

"Maggie I have been looking for someone to help me in my practice for almost three months. It will only be part time to start with but it could possibly lead to full time." Doc fumbled through his wallet and found his very last business card. "I have to carry more of these with me," Doc thought, "You never know when you might need one."

"Maggie, here is my business card. If you are interested in talking further about the position, please give me a call. We can set up an appointment for you to come in and see the office."

"Thanks, Doc."

For the past three months, Doc had been doing everything from performing the therapy to answering telephones, setting client appointments and doing billings. He desperately needed help. "I certainly hope Maggie calls," Doc kept saying to himself as he shredded another HCFA 1500 insurance form with the wrong billing code typed incorrectly. Doc's typing skills were marginal. Making appointments and doing all of his own intakes were starting to exact a toll, as Doc had not been able to take a day off for those three months and was starting to feel the effects of it. He found himself going to bed earlier each night. He was exhausted by the time he got home, and sometimes just collapsed in bed with his clothes on. Doc had not been out in months.

Doc was leaving the bathroom when he heard the phone ring and quickly walked to the reception area to answer it. "If I don't get it on the fourth ring it goes to voice mail," Doc mumbled, and he picked it up on the third ring.

"Hello, this is Doc."

"Hello Doc, this is Maggie and I wanted to see if you might be available to meet me tomorrow."

"Maggie, how does 1:00 p.m. sound, right after lunch?"

"That will be perfect Doc. I can't wait to see the office. Goodbye."

Walking back from lunch, Doc was thinking about his interview with Maggie that day. "Fourth floor, please," he instructed the elevator operator. As he opened the door, he saw Maggie sitting in the waiting room.

"Maggie how are you today?"

"Doc I am doing great today."

"Please come in."

"Doc I really like the office. The décor is very dark but I like the location. It is so convenient for me from my house in Sausalito. It only took me 30 minutes to get here this afternoon."

"Maggie, don't count on that daily, as the commute time can change like the wind. Trust me, I know from personal experience. Let me show you around."

Doc noticed that Maggie would stop and jot down notes in a small notebook she was carrying while she walked down the hall toward Doc's office. He had no idea what she was writing down but he would find out later when the movers came.

"Doc, I like the physical layout of your office."

"Why?"

"Your office is down the hall from the waiting room, which gives you and the patients privacy. You also have a back door where the patients can exit without seeing someone they might know in your waiting room. If you would like, Doc, I could help you with a little decorating. I think we could repaint the office a brighter color, maybe a tan or mauve. I would recommend getting a new leather couch and wing back chair for your office and new chairs for the waiting room. I think tan would look better than the black you have now. Clients would like that better." Doc noted that Maggie certainly was a take charge person.

"Maggie, we will hold off of on the decorating for now."

Before he could ask Maggie the first question she blurted out, "Doc, I am planning on enrolling in the Master of Arts Counseling program as a part-time student in the evening at the University of California in the fall of 1999. I know that working part- time for you would give me a limited view of what happens in a mental health setting."

"Maggie, the only experience I could provide you with would be clerical. I would need for you to set appointments, answer the telephone, bill insurance companies, and make bank deposits."

"Doc, not a problem. When would you want me to start?"

"Maggie, I like your enthusiasm but I would like for you to complete an application first. Please list three professional work references and also give me permission to do a background check. Also, if I hire you I can only pay you $15 an hour to begin with and I will re-evaluate your progress in 90 days."

"Doc, the salary is fine," she said as she handed him a thoroughly completed application that she finished in ten minutes. Doc was already impressed with her attention to detail and her speed.

"Maggie, I will call you with my decision by the end of the week."

A week had gone by and Doc was still waiting for the last reference Maggie listed to return his call. He wanted to make his decision quickly, but needed to temper his zeal.

"I want to make a good hiring decision for my office and my clients. I have to be thorough, like Maggie." Maggie would be the first person clients would meet. Some of them had never come to a therapist's office in their life. Maggie would be the first impression they would have so her demeanor and competence was very important as it would also initially communicate a good first impression to clients about the staff, office and the practice. Any receptionist had to be personable, not easily frustrated, professional at all times, always show respect to the clients and always maintain their confidentiality.

Putting away some client files, Doc heard the phone ring and rushed to get it before it went to voicemail. It was after hours. "I hope this isn't a client emergency," Doc thought.

"Hello this is Doc can I help you?"

"Doc, this is Doctor Wenton Brown from Brown Health Center in Chicago. I got your message that you wanted to know about Maggie Wendt's working with us." The first words out of Doctor Brown's mouth were, "HIRE HER!!!!!!!!!!!!!"

"Doctor Brown, thank you for your enthusiastic comment but could I ask you a couple of questions? How long did Maggie work for you?"

"Over four years, and we hated to see her leave but her husband got an incredible job in San Francisco. We understood why she had to leave."

"Doctor Brown what was her position with you?"

"She was our receptionist, office manager, biller, and she even redecorated the offices on her own. She did everything, and has an incredible eye for colors. We have a general practice treating many emotional disorders. Our staff includes five psychiatrists, including myself, three licensed clinical social workers, and two child psychologists. We probably see between 300 and 400 patients weekly. Maggie was never late and rarely called in sick and is absolutely wonderful with clients. I recommend her highly for any job involving working with the public."

"Thank you, Doctor Brown, for your comments. They have helped me to make my decision. Thanks again for your call."

"Doc, before I say goodbye please tell Maggie we send our best to her from Chicago."

Doc was smiling as he hung up the phone. "I guess it was now my lucky day," Doc thought. He had decided to ask Maggie to join him in the practice. "I only hope that my small practice would be able to offer her the experiences she's looking for."

"Hello, is Maggie Wendt there?"

"This is Maggie Wendt. Oh, hi Doc!"

"Maggie, are you still interested in working with me?"

"Yes!!!" Maggie said, almost yelling in my ear.

"Can you be here next Monday at 9:00 a.m.? I can start training you on billings, and other duties."

"I want the job Doc, and yes I will be there prompt next Monday at 9:00 a.m."

Walker Smith and Mr. Atlas

Maggie had been with Doc for over two weeks and knew most of what was needed to make the office run and what needed to be done. What a gem. Doc was even persuaded to have the office professionally painted and also ordered new, light colored furniture that looked great. Maggie had been right about the way clients would like it and even Doc began to look forward to the bright colors of the office whenever he came to work.

"Doc, this is Maggie. Are you all right? I just got your message. I just got into the office."

"Traffic is a nightmare, Maggie. I am stuck in this traffic and don't know when I will be in. I have a 9:00 a.m. appointment with Walker Smith. Please call him and see if he wants to reschedule."

"Will do," she said as she hung up.

Doc looked at his watch and realized that he had only traveled 300 feet in 30 minutes. It was now 8:00 a.m., and there was no relief in sight on the bridge. He would never make the 9:00 o'clock session. Doc kept humming, "I left my heart in another traffic nightmare in San Francisco." This definitely wasn't California dreaming.

Finally the traffic started to move and the morning sun was starting to peek through the fog. Doc made good time coming across the bridge and exceeded the speed limit just a little going down Market Street to his office on California Street.

"All I have left to do is park my car and then run fast for two city blocks, and I should be on time for my first appointment." Doc hoped that Murphy's Law wouldn't apply today.

"Fourth floor please," Doc panted to the elevator operator. Looking at his watch, Doc couldn't believe it was only 8:58 a.m. He had two minutes to spare. As he turned the door knob, he saw Maggie typing and a man sitting slouched over, reading the morning paper.

"Doc, Walker Smith is here. I couldn't reach him after we last spoke."

"Maggie, give me five minutes to get my breath," Doc whispered to her, feeling very short-winded.

"Walker good morning, my name is Doc." Doc extended his hand to shake Walker's, and he handed him his completed intake form with trembling hands. His handshake was limp.

"Please come this way to my office." As Doc turned the knob to open the office door, he noticed in his peripheral vision that Walker was less than an inch away. Had Doc stopped suddenly, he would surely have bumped into his back. Walker was still trembling, only now Doc noticed the tremor a little more than when he first shook his hand in the waiting room.

"Walker, please come in and have a seat on the sofa." Before Doc began his initial assessment process, during which he identified the client's presenting problem and their strengths and weaknesses, Walker stated quietly, almost whispering, "Thanks for seeing me Doc, I am at my wits' end."

Walker Smith stated he was 35 and single on the intake form, had never been married and had no children or any family. His blue jeans and gray plaid flannel shirt appeared to be fresh from the cleaners. The white tennis shoes he wore appeared to be new, as there didn't seem to be a mark on them. Walker appeared to be at least six feet tall, with a medium build and light, sandy brown hair. He was favored with dazzling hazel eyes that sparkled when the sunlight shone upon them.

"Mr. Smith, please be seated."

"Please call me Walker." He appeared tense and anxious as he rocked back and forth on the couch. His speech was still in the whisper mode.

"Walker, what brings you in to see me? Could you please speak up a little bit?"

Suddenly elevating the tone of his voice, Walker started to recite his tale.

"I worked for a jerk who owned a psychiatric care facility. I was there for six months and he fired me in June of this year for no valid reason." His eyes reddened and tears started streaming down his cheek as he started to sob. Doc gave him a few minutes and then proceeded to ask, "Walker what specifically did they say you did?"

"I transferred an elderly male patient out of the health care facility who was caught preying on female patients. I was in charge of the facility and personally notified the police. My ex-boss said this was an internal matter and I did not have the authority to involve the police."

"It sounds like you did the right thing."

"If that is true, then why was I fired?"

"Walker, hopefully this process will start to provide you with some of those answers."

Walker's irritation grew as he continued telling his story. Doc and Walker were already thirty minutes into the first session, and it seemed to Doc that Walker was a man in great emotional distress who would need more than one or two sessions to work through some of his issues. Doc changed the focus of the session away from Walker's termination in an effort to reduce his apparent level of discomfort.

"Walker, how have you been sleeping and what is your appetite like?"

"I have only been sleeping three or four hours a night, and I have lost ten pounds in a month and have very little appetite." Walker got up off of the couch and started pacing back and forth across the green oval area rug in the office at a rapid pace. Maggie had picked this plush emerald green rug up at a garage sale in Tiburon. The color matched her eyes and looked like it had just been delivered from Persia fresh off of the looms.

"Doc, I am so worried about money and finding a new job," he anxiously stated. "I look every day for a job but no one will hire me. I am really worried about what I am going to do and I feel powerless." Walker looked fearful and kept pacing over the same path. "I wish I hadn't called the police. Then I wouldn't be in this situation."

"Walker, I want you to sit down and relax. Please close your eyes. I want you to take in slow breaths to a total of 5 breaths. I want you to be aware of your breathing in and out. Walker, are your ready?"

"Yes."

"1.....2.... 3.....4.... and 5. Breathe in real deep for the last breath. Walker, how do you feel?"

"A little light headed."

"Walker, that is good. The breathing helps to increase your blood flow. Stress can really damage your immune system and the breathing exercise can help to increase the blood flow in your body. Your immune system can be negatively affected by stress. When you are relaxed you are better able to fight off the negative effects of stress. I want you to do this breathing exercise two to three times a day in the next week before our next session. Let me call Maggie to see if I have an opening next Saturday when I can see you."

As Doc dialed the telephone, Walker appeared to be a little more relaxed than he was when he came in to the session.

"Maggie, can you give Mr. Smith an appointment for next week?"

"Yes, how about 10:00 a.m."

"Walker, will this time work for you?"

"Yes."

"Good, then I will see you next Saturday, and don't forget to do the breathing exercise you just learned to help you relax when you feel stressed. It will help you relax and could also help you sleep better. Maggie, be sure to put Walker on my calendar for next week."

"No problem, Doc."

"Doc, I can find my way out."

Walker was dealing with the loss of his job and was in the grief cycle. He appeared to be immobilized by a feeling of being powerless and his inability to fully grasp the reality of his situation. Doc couldn't assess fully during the first session how powerless he really felt due to his high level of acute stress, and how strong his denial of reality was as the result of his financial and emotional dependence on his former job. Walker needed to understand that grief was the natural emotional response to the loss of his job if he was to get better. He also had to understand and work through the five stages of grief, which are (1) denial, (2) anger, (3) bargaining, (4) despair, and (5) acceptance.

❧❧❧❧❧❧❧❧❧❧

"Doc, Walker is thirty minutes early for his 10:00 a.m. appointment."

"Maggie, thanks."

"Doc, don't forget your dinner engagement tonight."

"Maggie, what dinner? Oh, yes I forgot the alumni meeting flea market tonight at Fisherman's Wharf at 8:00." Doc's college alumni group began their annual fundraiser every year on November 28th. He wondered how much the organization would raise this year. Doc was always happy to help in raising money that went to aid struggling college students with their tuition costs. He was grateful for the help he got when he was a student. Doc knew he could not have completed his studies without the scholarship help he received 15 years ago.

Walking down the hall to the waiting area, Doc noticed a new yellow lamp. "Maggie must have bought this one to add even more brightness to the hallway." A new light yellow color of paint on the wall looked fresh. Maggie was thorough and as Dr. Brown had said, she did have an eye for colors.

"Walker, why don't you come on back to my office."

"Doc, the hallway is really bright. What did you do?"

"Maggie has been busy decorating again. Walker please come in and sit down." The leather on the new tan couch that Maggie had selected wafted its fragrance as Walker sat down.

"How was your Thanksgiving?"

"Doc, I had a good Thanksgiving and I did the breathing exercises. They really made a difference."

"Congratulations! It is your first tool in your tool box that will help you to begin to develop some healthy coping skills to deal with stressors in your life. Please continue to do the breathing exercises as often as possible. Walker, it truly is a gift that keeps on giving the more you do it."

Walker smiled and widened his hazel eyes. Doc could really see their brilliance for the first time as the sun light came shining into the office window after being obscured by the fog for a while. The fog sometimes took forever to burn off. Walker's eyes sparkled like fine cut crystal as they caught the morning sunlight. Doc noticed that Walker also had a light reddish hue to his hair and was a little gray around his temples, details which he hadn't noticed until now.

Walker was very relaxed and was wearing a deep blue double-breasted worsted wool suit with a white, button-down oxford shirt. He also was wearing the most stunning fire engine red and white polka dot tie that Doc had ever seen. He wore freshly polished black penny loafers that appeared new with the shine they had on and was wearing black silk socks. Walker looked like he was either a fashion model or he was ready to go to the opera. This was a huge change from the man Doc first met the week before who was wearing blue jeans, a plaid flannel shirt, white socks and white tennis shoes and who was very anxious. After all, this was Saturday at 10:00 a.m. The way he was dressed, Doc speculated that he could have been going to the fund raiser as well that night.

"Doc, are you all right?"

Doc was still taking in the image of Walker, trying to figure out if there was any significance to it.

"Walker, you are very well dressed today. What is the occasion?"

"You are not going to believe this Doc, but I have a job interview after our session today. I am being interviewed for the director's position at a homeless shelter here in the Mission District."

"Walker, why don't you continue telling me how you came to work for Mr. Atlas?"

"Doc, I first met Mr. Atlas when he called me in for a job interview. I was very excited about working with the geriatric population, and his facilities were well known throughout the state for providing quality care to this client population. Mr. Atlas liked the fact that I had diverse experience running several small group care homes for schizophrenics for the state."

Doc noticed that, unlike Walker's last session, Walker appeared a little more relaxed and very animated as he continued telling his tale.

"Mr. Atlas thought that I could help his organization improve its image, which had been tarnished recently due to several complaints that had made the papers from the family members of some of the patients concerning alleged patient neglect. Mr. Atlas informed me that his attorneys said these were bogus charges and they had no merit. He thought by bringing me in that it could help his public relations with the community."

Walker continued, "One of the first things that Mr. Atlas wanted me to do was to speak to different health care facilities about the exceptional quality of care patients would receive at Mr. Atlas's geriatric care facility."

Walker's countenance changed slightly as he asked, "Why did Mr. Atlas fire me for notifying the authorities? I was just doing my job! He told me I put the organization and patients at great risk. I would never put patients at risk."

"Walker, we briefly touched on this in our last session. How do you feel about what he did?"

"I am angry."

"I want to help you resolve this loss, but I want you to claim your circumstances instead of letting them claim you. Do you understand that concept?"

"No I don't."

"Walker, do you think you did the right thing notifying the police?"

"Yes."

"If that is how you feel, then you have to claim the circumstances and be all right with what you did. It was the only thing you could do in the circumstances you found yourself in. Walker, you need to quit blaming yourself for what happened. Do you understand?"

"I think so, Doc."

"Walker, have you ever journaled?"

"No. I don't even know what that is."

"Walker, before you leave today and go to your interview I want to spend the remaining ten minutes we have introducing you to another tool that is going to be helpful to you to manage the stressors in your life. I want you to write in a journal every morning about the preceding day and bring it in on your next appointment. You will read it to me in the next session. This can help your therapy process move forward on a quicker pace as it helps me hear in your own words how you have managed your days. Journal writing can be useful for keeping track of a wide variety of things that can help you achieve your goals. I want you to use your journal to record your thoughts and feelings. 'Just doing it' can make a difference. Walker, by acknowledging underlying thoughts and feelings and writing about them, you can help you increase your self understanding and your self awareness which can make it easier for you to change your old patterns of behavior and to start new ones. Consistently keeping a journal is a strong message to yourself that you want to change and that you are committed to make it happen." Doc added, "One final instruction. I want you to write down three goals that you want to accomplish in the next six months. Make them as specific as possible. They should be realistic but challenging."

As Doc escorted Walker out of the office and down the bright hallway to the waiting area, he saw Maggie on the telephone and left her a note to give Walker an appointment for the 13th of December at 10:00 a.m.

"Good luck in your job interview," Doc remarked.

December 13th came, and Doc couldn't believe the rain that was falling that morning. The streets started to flood. Doc wished he had the opportunity to stay home.

"I wonder how many clients will cancel today because of the weather? Well, got to get up," Doc told himself as he hit the snooze button on the alarm for the third time.

As he entered the waiting room, Doc noticed that Walker was reading a magazine and appeared very relaxed and comfortable, as he had his feet up on the footstool and his tennis shoes were unlaced. Today he wore blue corduroy jeans, with a tan sweatshirt and his signature white tennis shoes.

"Walker, you look very relaxed today," Doc noted. "Please come on back to the office."

Walker walked in and sat down on the couch, and before Doc was able to sit down, he anxiously blurted out, "Doc, before we start can I tell you about a dream I had?"

Doc finally became situated in his chair and instructed Walker, "Go ahead and tell me about your dream."

"I saw boat docks of impressive yachts lining the San Francisco Bay, and Mr. Atlas had a lengthy dock at the end of which was a hangar-sized boat house. The highlights of my dream included viewing a thirty-eight foot Fountain Lightning which was speeding in the water and a forty-four foot Regal Commodore Cruiser which slept four, and I saw myself sleeping in this cruiser. I remember feeling simultaneously in awe and feeling nauseous while I was dreaming. I remember feeling unsteady as a non-seaman does walking the floating docks as my own free-floating anxiety rose. I remember seeing the name of his personal yacht, Narcissus Maximus."

"Mr. Atlas made me bow to his superior knowledge, superior wealth, and superior intelligence and also to his superiority. His office had a curved front bowing out to the hangar with one huge picture window surrounded by floor to ceiling reflecting mirrors. More mirrors were on the other walls as well. Wherever Atlas would be in the room, he could gaze at himself. I wanted to shake myself and wake up from this nightmare but it wasn't a nightmare. It felt so real. Doc, do you have any idea what this dream means?"

"Walker what do you think this means?"

"I don't know."

"Walker, let's begin with a simple definition of a dream."

A dream is a mental phenomenon occurring during sleep in which images, emotions, and thoughts are experienced with a sense of reality. The dreaming occurs during rapid eye movement sleep; typically there are four or five such periods a night having a total duration of about ninety minutes.

Doc asked, "Is this the first time you have had this dream?"

"Yes, Doc it is the first time I had this dream and it happened right after our first session."

"Walker you had what I call a compensatory dream. This dream of yours seems to have a content that is surprising to you. A dream that is compensatory helps counterbalance failings and needs. You seeing yourself on Mr. Atlas yacht and sleeping on the yacht, feeling in awe and nauseous would be a counterbalance to you feeling powerless and financially constrained right now."

"Doc that makes sense."

"Some therapists also believe that each of us is driven by a desire for power and our dreams reflect these ambitions." Doc thought for a moment, and continued, "Walker, I want you to write down the dream you just told me about. I want you to read it over carefully and see if you can find any significant connection with your situation and this dream. If you do I want you to write them down and bring with you on your next session. I will see you in two weeks. I think this was a good session for you today."

"Yea, Doc now it is starting to make a little bit of sense to me. I feel less angry today and I haven't cried. Just coming here and talking to you is amazing. I guess this is starting to help."

"Walker, dreams can be very useful to help us understand how our subconscious works out stressors that flood our minds daily."

Doc walked Walker out the back exit. He suddenly remembered that Maggie was off that day and he was all alone in the office, just like old times.

"Walker, please call Maggie on Monday and make an appointment to see me before Christmas. I am all alone today as she is off today doing Christmas shopping for her kids. I can't find the appointment book anywhere."

"Not a problem Doc, I will give her a call on Monday."

"Silent Night, Holy Night...."

Doc heard the carolers singing as he walked down the steps of the stopped cable car to exit and walk the two blocks to his office. Doc felt he was so lucky to get an office on California Street. The clients liked the location as it was easy to get to, and there was a parking garage only two blocks away. The landlord let him validate clients' parking fees as part of the rent he paid monthly.

Doc decided to take public transportation to work as the crowds of shoppers were immense and holiday traffic was a congested nightmare from six in the morning to rush hour. It reminded Doc of the traffic congestion on the Golden Gate that he was snarled in before, and he didn't want to go through that again. Doc knew he had a light day - only three patients in the morning - and planned to use the remainder of his Saturday to do Christmas shopping, then catch a quick bus ride back to Sausalito.

Doc couldn't believe that Christmas was on Monday in only three days. He still hadn't done any shopping. As Doc walked up the street, he noticed how beautiful the Embarcadero was with all of the colorful holiday decorations. He tried to imagine how many lights it took to light the Bay Bridge and Golden Gate Bridge at night. "I don't think I can count that high," Doc marveled. "What a beautiful sight when you come into the city at night with the bridges lit up." It truly was Christmas time in San Francisco.

Doc walked up California Street to his office and prepared mentally for his session with Walker. "I have to make sure that I help him stay focused to finish telling me his whole story." Doc sometimes let clients take him down several roads in order to build rapport with them, but then he would have to intervene and redirect their efforts before they both got lost.

"Fourth floor, please." As the elevator door opened he saw Walker going into the office. He was 45 minutes early for his appointment today. Doc made a note to tell him about this and to tell him that helplessness is the hallmark of trauma and empowerment is the antidote.

"Good morning Doc. Good morning Maggie."

"Doc, I don't know why Walker is here so early for his appointment. He called me on the Monday after his last appointment as he said you instructed him to do and I told him the first appointment you had today was at 10:00 a.m. He said he might be in a little early but I had no idea it would be almost an hour."

"Don't worry about it Maggie. I will be out to get him a few minutes before his appointment. I have to review his treatment plan and use the time to discuss it with him again."

Walking down the hall to the waiting room, Doc noticed that the yellow lamp was gone and there was now a lime green lamp in its place. It looked very good in the hallway.

"Mr. Smith are you ready?"

"Yes."

"Come on back to my office so we can begin."

Before Doc could turn around, Walker bolted out in front of him and quickly walked down the hall and had the door open to the office before Doc was halfway down the hall. He appeared very eager to get the session started.

"Walker, we have only one goal today in our session and that is for you to finish telling me your whole story with Mr. Atlas and his company. Why don't you start as to why you think he hired you."

"Doc, Mr. Atlas was facing financial liquidity issues as expected funding from the insurance companies were being withheld to his corporation. He couldn't make payroll, his patient referrals were down from psychiatric hospitals in the community and the health care governing board had temporarily suspended his operating license as a residential care facility. The insurance companies also had temporarily suspended funds due to the facility and any other future billings to his organization until he resolved all complaints successfully and got his operating license reinstated. The situation was hurting his company financially."

"Walker, please continue."

"Mr. Atlas told me that I could help him get his health care clinics in compliance with regulations which would help to release revenue from the insurance companies. I still remember meeting him for the first time. I was struck by the opulence of his office. He had entered the waiting room shortly after I'd gotten comfortable in one of the many leather couches in his 300-square foot waiting room. He wore three glittering gold necklaces and also wore a multi-rubied Rolex yellow gold watch that gleamed as he held the chronograph facing the crystal chandelier in the waiting room. He had noticed after I shook his hand that I was looking at his Rolex watch. He asked me if I liked it. 'Yes, sir' I told him, and he said this timepiece cost twenty-three K plus."

Walker continued, "His office was incredible. He had expensive hardwood flooring throughout the palatial office. I am sure it cost more than I would have earned in a year. The Steinway baby grand stood open in the corner. He had a full-sized Adler pool table that stood in another corner. He'd told me his hand carved, diamond studded cue was a gift from the governor of a neighboring state; the governor offered it as an incentive in order to help get one of his relatives a room sooner. Atlas said he told the governor he'd need a table to use the cue on, and its presentation helped to seal an immediate placement for a specified person. He'd also told me the amounts paid for the Picasso and Rockwell paintings hanging behind his desk. If you didn't ask the prices of his objects he told you."

"Walker, thanks for the great details about Mr. Atlas but could we now talk about the specifics related to the incident at the health care facility?"

"Sure Doc, but first I have to give you some history. I will make up names to protect these patients so you can understand how the story flows."

"I understand."

"Mrs. Gee was an elderly resident, handicapped, and wheelchair bound. She had a sweet smile but talked very little. A short stroll with the staff in the sunshine would make her beam. She was the favorite resident of most of the staff at SRN, which I would add, was a highly capable and compassionate staff. Mr. Ess, on the other hand, also got extra attention but that was because he should not have been there. As I mentioned before, Mr. Atlas liked his fancy pool cue and expensive table. That is the only reason elderly Mr. Ess was there as he was related to the Governor's wife. He should have been in a geriatric locked criminal unit. Other residents' lost jewelry would frequently be found in his room. Mr. Ess knew from whom he could steal; which residents were alert to details, which ones had the poorest memories."

"One weekend night while I was off duty, Mr. Ess knew we were short-staffed and made his most heinous move. Ms. Elcee, our nurse, was the only staff member present for a few hours. We were within state regulations for coverage due to the number of patients on the unit during sleeping hours, but I preferred to have at least one more staff member around. While all was quiet on the ward in the early morning, Ess entered Gee's room while she slept soundly. Then he lifted her blanket and gown, dropped his pants, and entered Mrs. Gee."

"Nurse Elcee heard Mrs. Gee's muffled whines from well down the hall. She interrupted Mr. Ess by yelling at him. He pulled his penis out slowly, according to Nurse Elcee's notes, patted Mrs. Gee's bottom affectionately, pulled up his pajama pants, and walked calmly back to his own room. The nurse reported that Mrs. Gee sat sobbing quietly in her arms for almost an hour before falling back to sleep."

"When I came into the facility Monday morning, I was informed of the incident and immediately went into action. I considered this a criminal action and called the police. Mrs. Gee was sent to the hospital for evaluation and treatment of both her emotional violation and her sexual assault. Mr.

Ess was expelled from the home as the prosecuting attorney was going to file criminal charges for sexual assault. Mr. Ess had no medical history of senile dementia and he knew exactly what he was doing. My staff cheered my actions. Mrs. Gee's children applauded my care for their mother."

"I heard through the grapevine at the corporate office the Governor called Mr. Atlas and bitched about his relative being out on his own at age eighty-three. Yours truly got screamed at next. Mr. Atlas summoned me to his office and screamed at me. He said, 'Where the hell are your priorities? Fix this mess, Mr. Smith and fix it now!' I told him that I refused to re-admit Mr. Ess."

"I told him that a rape had been committed in his facility and I wasn't going to have a rapist as a patient and put other patients and staff at risk. Mr. Atlas really got upset then. I had gotten the support of the Medical Director of the corporation, and the Director of Nursing, the police, and a state agency that oversaw medical facilities commended my interventions. This infuriated him."

"Mr. Atlas was still screaming and pounding his fist on the African mahogany desk in his office. He shouted, 'Your first obligation is to make us money, not report alleged rapes. Walker I don't know why the hell you are so upset. Rapes happen everyday in mental health care facilities."

I replied, "Sir, with all due respect, the rape was witnessed by a nurse so it is not alleged, and I have a sworn affidavit of what she witnessed that is signed and notarized."

"He then proceeded to sit down and continued yelling at me. 'I'll get right to the point, Walker. Get your ass out of my office and out of my organization. You are fired. Oh, and don't even try to use me as a reference for another job, especially in this town. We'll send your personal stuff to your home.'"

"Doc, that's my story. I found out that Mr. Ess was readmitted the same day I got fired with the personal approval of Mr. Atlas, and he was escorted from jail to the facility by Mr. Atlas' personal driver. Mr. Gee's husband dropped the rape charges because Mrs. Gee was very frail, and he was afraid that the stress of a trial might kill her. I can only assume she got an extra blanket and free care for a while by the staff for the minimum number of days needed to get everyone satisfied again."

"Doc, there is one more thing. I received a call from a U.S. Senator three months after I was fired. He is up for re-election and is currently wanting to investigate the quality of patient care in health care facilities throughout the state. Senator Merson told me that a patient at one of Atlas's facilities was found dead from what was deemed denial of basic care. How senseless! How greedy! How unnecessary and sad. I told the Senator I would help him in any way I could, so Mr. Atlas could not hurt others and their families with poor care. He has asked me to testify before his committee in Washington next year."

As Walker finished his story, Doc mused, "How unfortunate and sad that this patient and maybe others had to be subjected to abuse just because of Mr. Atlas's unethical behavior and his obsessive drive for money at any costs." As Walker had so eloquently said - how senseless! How greedy! How unnecessary and how sad!

The uncaring and obviously self-centered nature of Mr. Atlas is a great illustration of the narcissist. He lacked empathy and seemed to be totally absorbed with his own self-image, which precluded him from being concerned with the feelings of others.

As the session ended, Walker smiled with a big grin and said, "Thanks for today. Merry Christmas, Happy New Year and by the way, I have to leave town and will be gone for two to three weeks. I have some interviews on the east coast from the middle of January and will be back in California on February 8th. I am also going to meet with Senator Merson at the end of my trip on February 5th and 6th in his Washington D.C. office to work on the investigation that he has launched."

"Walker, please continue journaling and bring your work with you at your next appointment. I will see you on the second Saturday in February at 10:00 a.m. and by the way, Merry Christmas to you and a very blessed New Year. Good luck on the interviews and with the Senator."

It was already the middle of February, 1999. Doc turned the knob on the door and walked into the office door and saw Walker looking pensive.

He had a faraway look in his hazel eyes, as if in a dream state. He was Doc's first client of the day, and Doc figured he might have a lot to talk about.

"Walker, welcome back. Please come on down to my office so we can begin your session. Please sit down. How was your trip and how did your job interviews go?"

"Fine, but I am not feeling very well. I have been sick with an upset stomach, I have a headache and I can't sleep."

"Would you like to re-schedule when you are feeling better?"

Walker replied, "No. I need to see you today."

"Please tell me about your trip."

Walker was quiet and then said, "Mr. Atlas took all of my power. He fired me. I don't have a job, I don't have any money saved, I have a house payment due, and I haven't told anyone in my family what happened. You are the only person who knows." Walker sobbed as he uttered, "What am I to do? What am I to do?" Walker yelled, "That asshole should be arrested and I want to be the one who takes him down!"

Doc felt the session being hijacked and he knew he had to redirect Walker's attention to get focus back on the session.

"Walker let's talk about how you feel at this moment."

"How the hell is that supposed to help me Doc? I feel angry, alone and frustrated by this situation."

"Do you feel that Mr. Atlas fired you for poor work performance?"

"No, absolutely not. I was doing an excellent job for him and I had really worked on improving the care and reducing costs without having patient care suffer. I thought he was happy with what he was seeing from me."

"Walker why do you feel Mr. Atlas fired you?"

"Because I reported a rape at the facility and it added to the negative publicity his corporation was already receiving."

"Walker, Mr. Atlas is probably not capable of being empathetic to you or anyone. The one thing you can change now at this moment is the way you are reacting to Mr. Atlas's behaviors. You have to take your power back and be the one who is having the experience, not be the object of the experience."

"Walker, you are probably feeling very frustrated, all alone and having to fend for yourself, and you are angry. Walker, Mr. Atlas might not have wanted your feedback or a critique on the incident, but only for you to provide a positive reflection of him."

"Walker, your choice was either to make Mr. Atlas look good or to do the right thing. You chose the latter, and you reaped the consequences that come when you go up against someone who is totally vested in looking good, rather than being good. Walker, how would you have felt if you had covered the rape up and stayed silent?"

"Doc, I could never lower myself to something as loathsome as that even if it meant losing my job."

"Walker, after viewing these options does it help you to be able to accept and embrace the reality of this situation?"

"Doc, you are absolutely right. I did the right thing."

"Walker, before we end today, let's have you do your breathing exercise. Are you ready? Breathe in with deep breaths – one, inhale and then exhale, 2...3...4...5." Doc recognized that Walker finally had gotten through the whole story and was starting to accept the reality of his situation.

"Walker, I want to see you in two weeks. In our next session time, we are going to go over your journal and talk about your future job prospects and your trip, which we didn't have time to get to today. We also might begin to have you start to work on understanding your grief cycle. Good work today, Walker. See you in two weeks, and tell Maggie as you leave to give you an appointment for the first of March."

As Doc drove home, he remembered some words of wisdom one of his clinical supervisors and mentors had taught him years ago. "We have to gladly embrace and do therapy with humility at all times, and to always ensure that clients feel safe. Our clients are asked to become deeply vulnerable in therapy to another human being, and to allow many disturbing feelings and thoughts to be expressed. A therapist has to convince them that this is absolutely necessary to their healing. The client must have a strong feeling of trust in you as their therapist. They must feel safe." Doc used that guidance as his barometer of the quality of care he provided. He was pretty sure that Walker felt safe in therapy. He was starting to deal with many of his disturbed feelings and was expressing his thoughts freely in his sessions, and he was starting to get better.

A good therapist recognizes when a client can be pushed and when support is necessary. When to cry with the client and when to laugh at life. . . .when to push a client to accept responsibility, and when to help him recognize himself as blameless. . . when to accept and when to challenge. Each of these stances is a means to meeting the client's goals. Doc was determined that Walker, like all of his clients, would get the best therapy he could provide. Having these stances framed above the door of Doc's office was a constant reminder to him of how important humility was for a good therapist.

"Maggie, were you able to verify all of my appointments for this Saturday?"

"Everyone confirmed except Mr. Walker Smith, but I left a message for him on his voice mail. I am sure he won't miss the appointment, as he never has yet."

Doc waved farewell to another client, and he said, "Ms. Berton, please make another appointment with Maggie. I will see you again in three weeks. Keep journaling. You are really starting to develop more insight into your issues." Doc walked her down the hall out to the waiting area where Maggie was and where she kept the appointment book "Be careful outside, the winds have really kicked up."

"Doc, Walker is on the phone."

"Hello Mr. Smith, are you on your way? It is almost 12:30."

"No I am on the way to the airport. Senator Merson wants me in Washington by Monday to testify against Mr. Atlas and his organization. I have to go, and I will call you when I get back in town next week."

As Walker walked through the mahogany doors to enter Senator Merson's office, he thought it was deja vu for a moment. The senator's office had expensive hardwood flooring and was subtly opulent. The only thing he didn't have was a Steinway baby grand and a full-sized Adler pool table standing in a corner. He wondered if Atlas and the senator shared the same decorator.

"Mr. Smith, thanks for coming," Senator Merson's aide greeted Walker. "Please follow me to the committee chambers where Senator Merson is waiting for you and where you will give your testimony."

Walker couldn't believe how overwhelming the room was. The senators looked like gods frowning down from Mount Olympus behind their Honduran mahogany desks.

"Please raise your right hand to be sworn."

After one hour of grueling testimony telling the committee about the incident, Walker was excused and Senator Merson thanked him. His aide escorted Walker out of the regal chamber.

Walker remembered Doc told him to journal, and he realized that this was a good experience to write about. "Monday, 1st Monday in March 1999," Walker wrote, "I testified before nine senators today, and I am feeling vindicated. I think this is what I needed to do and it is a noble act I have performed. I was a voice for the poor patients that are never heard. I hope that my testimony can prevent some other unfortunate patient from getting hurt out of someone's greed. Maybe this was part of that grief cycle Doc talked about. I didn't feel like I was in denial anymore, and no longer felt angry or trying to bargain, and I know I didn't feel despair. Maybe I had moved into acceptance. I suddenly felt new meaning in living and I wasn't afraid. I had taken action as I flew across the country to tell my story and I definitely had shared this with others."

A piece of paper fell out of Walker's journal. It was a note from Doc to Walker. "Please read before you journal daily. Remember Walker, grief is defined as a normal process and reaction to a loss. The loss may be physical (such as a death), social (such as a divorce) or occupational (such as a job)."

"Emotional reactions of grief can include anger, guilt, anxiety, sadness, and despair. Physical reactions of grief can include sleeping problems, changes in appetite, physical problems such as chronic pain or illness.

The five stages of grief are:

- Denial
- Anger

- Bargaining
- Depression
- Acceptance

I hope this helps as you journal – Doc."

"Maybe I can get some sightseeing in before I have to fly back to San Francisco tomorrow," Walker thought. "The Senator's office said his aide could drive me around to some of the sights if I wanted. Why not? I can't wait to see Doc next week and tell him all about my journey."

Easter was upon us, and business had been slow but that was a welcome relief for Doc. It was Saturday, and it was the first time in two years that there wasn't one appointment on the books. Maggie and Doc planned to catch up on paperwork.

"Doc, the mailman just delivered a letter that just came in special delivery."

"Please bring it back. Who is it from, Maggie?"

"It is post marked from Oxford, England and I think it is from Mr. Walker Smith." As Maggie handed Doc the letter, he dropped it, anxiously trying to open it to see how Walker had been. Doc had not heard from him or seen him since he left for Washington.

"Doc, I must thank you for all of your support and guidance. I constantly share with others all that you have done for me. They know you all too well. You and others encouraged me and supported me. I have talked to one former co-worker and they said that I gave them hope to start over with a whole new life."

"I realized that many people are scared to take a chance at being something different. Starting over can be scary, most people don't like change. I had no choice it seems or did I? I am so excited to be in England. It is a dream job and I still can't believe they hired me to run two of their 100 bed health care homes. I got the call in D.C. and never did come back to San Francisco. It is different over here as everyone receives the same kind of care regardless of their ability to pay. I only have to answer to a board of directors and none of them are owners as it is a government facility. No rumors, no negativity, at least not yet, Ha Ha."

"I surround myself with positive and motivated people, both at church and at work. I never believed I would work in such a wonderful and beautiful environment."

"I continue to use your exercises, such as breathing exercises, journaling and I read everyday before I journal the words about what grief is. This has helped me to understand where I am at on my journey. People have commented on my energy. I didn't know I was giving any off. I have met several women who I am interested in dating but still feel that's a step that can wait. I have gained some weight and it hurts the self esteem but I know what I need to do."

"I just wanted to share my good fortune with you because after all you have been with me from the beginning. And now it seems I am closing the chapter on a really bad and nightmarish episode of my life. I feel great now. I am more clear on my future, more focused and determined to get out there and succeed but I know I have a long way to go before I am 100% and fully independent. I now rely on my new friends to vent and use as a crutch when I feel the hopelessness. Again, it's a road I am on for the long haul."

"Once again, thanks Doc, I couldn't have gotten this far in life without your assistance and concern. I will keep you posted, and oh by the way, Mr. Atlas and his staff were indicted by the government and he pled guilty. He was sentenced to a year in prison and no probation. The blessing is that he can no longer be involved in any part of the health care business or with patients for the rest of his life. Kind regards, Walker."

Doc never saw Walker again for therapy, as he never came back to America. Walker gathered the strength he needed and came to therapy to make the choice to change his life and take his power back. Walker reports via email periodically that he is doing very well in Oxford and in his life. He accesses therapy occasionally as a check up and still journals and does the relaxation exercises Doc taught him when he remembers to. One recent e-mail read, "Doc, I acted ethically and with integrity, and I am able to sleep at nights. I might have suffered financially but I have been blessed and I ain't wearing an orange jumpsuit. I have realized that outcomes depend on our choices we make in life. I am satisfied but I still have a ways to go. Happy Easter, Doc."

Doc smiled and logged off the computer. He turned the lights off, and thought that the e-mail served to remind him of his purpose.

"Have a great Easter Maggie, with your family. I am going home to mine now."

Avoiding Life

As Doc was driving to his office, he was struck by the fact that he was not in bumper to bumper traffic for the usual Monday morning commute on the Golden Gate Bridge into San Francisco. Was this a dream?

"Tomorrow is July 4th and a lot of people probably took off for a four day holiday weekend," Doc said to himself. "I have been living in San Francisco almost two years. I can't believe it is already July 4, 2000. Where did the time go?"

Doc's office was still the one on California Street. He hoped that the landlord would never sell the building or that some new developer would come down to raze the building. He believed he was safe for a while. This was the perfect location for his practice, and the clients loved it. Maggie had cut down her hours from a full 40-hour work week to working three eight-hour days, as she was now enrolled in the graduate program in counseling. It was a tough adjustment, but Doc couldn't think of having anyone else work with him in the office with clients. He was more than willing to make the needed adjustments. Doc had to come in on Saturdays every three weeks in order to stay caught up while Maggie took classes, but she was out for summer break now, and Doc could stop doing that, at least until September.

Doc was so happy to have weekends free again during the summer. He planned to do some more hiking in Muir Woods and in Big Basin with his family whenever they would want to visit from out of town. He also enjoyed hiking with friends. This served as a mini vacation, and was only a short thirty to forty-five minute drive from Doc's home and office.

The spring or summer had always been Doc's favorite times to go connect with nature in the woods. Doing this really helped clear Doc's head, especially when he took Mitzi, as she would lead him down trails he would normally not go down. They always came back to where they had started. Mitzi's instincts and her sense of smell were incredible. Doc believed he could never get lost with her. Mitzi would wag her tail incessantly on Saturday mornings to let Doc know she was ready to go, she so loved the outdoors and hiking. She would jump into the Bronco without any encouragement and Doc thought she would drive it if he gave her the keys. Her head would be out the back window as soon as it was rolled down. She loved the wind blowing in her face and the cool air as they would come into Big Basin with all of the redwoods. The smells were awesome. She was in her zone.

Doc came back to reality when he entered the office on Monday.

"Doc, how was your weekend?"

"Great Maggie! I was able to go hiking in Big Basin with Mitzi. She makes me laugh and smile when she is chasing squirrels. Maggie how about your weekend?"

"Very good. My husband will be able to spend time with me and the kids all summer. He doesn't have any travel plans for his job."

"That sounds like it was great timing for you as you are off of school."

"I am excited as he can spend more time with the kids by himself."

"If you need any extra time off during the summer to spend with your family please let me know."

"Thanks Doc and I just might take you up on your generous offer."

"Maggie, what's the day look like for us today?"

"You only have three morning appointments - at 9, 10, and 11. Doc, I have gotten all of the billings done for June and have done all of the bank deposits. You have pretty full days on Wednesday through Friday of this week. Oh, and we got a call this morning from a new client. Mr. John Burton was referred to you and you will never guess by whom," Maggie rattled off.

"Who?"

"Mr. Walker Smith."

"Really? We haven't heard anything from Mr. Smith for over a year. I wonder how is he doing?"

"I know that is why I was surprised as well."

"Maggie, after the last appointment let's call it a day."

A big smile creased Maggie's face. "That sounds good to me. My husband and I can get some sparklers for the kids for tomorrow. I won't allow them to have firecrackers but sparklers are fine, and they get so excited when we go in the backyard and light them up. The kids just love the way they sparkle in the air when they move them around in circular motions."

"When do you have Mr. Burton scheduled for his first appointment?"

"Next Monday, July 10th at 10:00 a.m. Doc, I also told him to be here early to fill paperwork out so you could begin at 10:00 a.m. sharp."

"Mr. Burton good morning. Did you have any trouble finding the office?"

"No," he quietly said, handing Doc the clipboard with all of the insurance forms filled out completely. Doc extended his hand for a handshake, but Mr. Burton did not extend his own. Doc was struck instantly by his reluctance to shake his hand and also the legibility of the forms he completed. He printed in very small letters. It was very hard to read.

"Mr. Burton, please follow me down the hall to my office and we can get started." As Doc walked down the hall with the client, he noticed the answer to the question "What brings you to therapy?" was odd. Mr. Burton had answered, "Get fixed." Doc thought silently to himself about how clients spend their lives self-destructing and when they become fearful or tired of feeling out of sync, they want an instant fix. It brought to mind the image of an elephant in their living room. They have been walking around the elephant most of their lives. It didn't move in overnight and it wasn't going to vanish overnight by opening the door to therapy. The typical client gets frightened when they start to bump into it. Once they are told they have the power to rid themselves of the elephant, they get excited until some of them realize the hard work and tenacity it takes to get rid of it by eating it a bite at a time. Some never come back through the door, as they are either not eager to do the work, or they don't want to devote the time it takes to "eat the elephant." Many use the excuse, "My appetite isn't that big."

John Burton's intake form stated he was a 44 year old single male with a daughter somewhere. He was married once when he was 16 years of age and divorced at 21. He also reported that he had no relationship at all with his daughter, and didn't know where she lived.

"Mr. Burton, is this the first time you have been in therapy?"

"Doc, you can call me John. Doc, to answer your question, no. I am a recovering alcoholic. My recovery has been fraught with many potholes, and I have had my share of broken axles and flat tires."

Doc was surprised by the picturesque description of his recovery.

"My life has been full of making bad choices. I want to get fixed! Doc, I have decided that I am going to give therapy one more chance to see if it can help me. A good friend of mine, Walker Smith, said you could help me. He certainly turned his life around and I know he was seeing you. He would call me after some of the sessions and encourage me to call you. It has taken me a year to make that call. I can't disappoint Walker; he has been so good to me since I have been in San Francisco. I want to surprise him. He even let me crash at his house for a week after my drunken girlfriend threw me out. I promised him that I would come over to visit him this year in England. I don't want to be like I am now because I would never get on the plane."

"John, how would you describe the way you feel now?"

"I don't like being around people socially and when I am I get panic attacks and start freaking out. I can't even imagine being on a plane for ten hours surrounded by people. What if they want to talk to me? I wouldn't know what to do but panic."

"John, tell me what you do professionally. I see on your intake form that you put down 'tradesman.' Could you be a little more specific?"

"Yeah, I am a master plumber and have been for twenty years. I can work alone and don't have to interact with anyone. I wish my boss would just let me do my job."

"Why do you say that?"

"He is always wanting me to participate in meetings with customers, or to make presentations to customers. Every time he wants to do my annual evaluation I usually call in sick, and have done that for the past several years. The most recent evaluation he scheduled was for last Monday morning. I ended up in the emergency room at the hospital the day before on Sunday night with a serious panic attack, and they kept me. I didn't get out until this Tuesday morning. I haven't been able to sleep more than two hours a night and I have lost ten pounds in three weeks. Doc, I haven't got a raise in the two years I have worked. My boss recommended that I should see a counselor after this recent incident in the hospital. He wants to keep me on, but he is getting worried now about what I might do on a job site. He doesn't want me to freak out and walk away from the work site. My boss, Mr. Wilson, tries and keeps me from having to interact with other people as much as possible as he knows how this makes me react, and he says it can be bad for business. He says he can't continue rescuing me from myself."

John paused for a moment, then continued, "Doc, I don't need a raise. I am happy just the way things are."

"John, let's leave this issue for now. Tell me about your parents."

"They divorced when I was sixteen and my mother worked two jobs to pay the bills. Dad didn't provide any support when he walked out on us. I didn't hear from him or see him for a year, and then it was by accident."

"John, what do you mean?"

"I had gotten a part-time job at a local grocery store as a clerk stocking shelves to help my mother out with my school clothes. My Dad approached me one day and said, 'How are you doing, John?' I was in shock. I was angry and wanted to tell him to leave me alone. I was paralyzed. I didn't know what to do at that moment and became panicked. I remember feeling very hot and was perspiring. My breathing became labored and I started to hyperventilate. I stopped it by breathing into a bag. I always carry one with me as I never know when I will need one."

"What happened then?"

"Dad continued to talk about living in the neighborhood and shopping in the store often for groceries with Carol. Carol, he told me was his new girl. He asked me to give him a call sometime so we could grab some beers. He gave me a card with his telephone number and left the store."

"What happened next?"

"I tore the card up and then went into the alley and threw up and the next thing I remember is my boss slapping my face and asking if I was all right." John became very quiet. "Doc, I am feeling nauseous."

"John, this is a good place to stop the session today. Let me show you to the bathroom."

Opening the office door, Doc escorted John out to the hall bathroom and waited outside the door. John came out in a couple of minutes with water dripping from his face.

"Doc, the cold water on the face always works."

"John, let's have Maggie give you an appointment for next week. Maggie, can you please give John an appointment for next week?"

"Not a problem."

"If you start to have any panic attacks during the week, call me."

After Doc closed his office door for lunch, he jotted down some goals for John's treatment plan in his file. Doc knew that John had to improve on his social interactions, he had to decrease his avoidant behavior, and he had to improve his self-esteem. He also knew that he had to focus the treatment as well, in order to reduce any therapeutic resistance John had by continuing to build on today's session, establishing a trusting therapeutic relationship. Doc didn't want to engage John too quickly nor did he want to pressure him with expectations. This elephant must be approached with caution, and eaten a bite at a time in small pieces.

Driving along Highway 101, Doc saw a rainbow and knew this was going to be a great day. He only had eight clients to see that day. "Maybe I will see one more," he mused.

As Doc pulled into the parking lot, he saw John sitting in his car and he appeared to be sleeping.

"What is he doing here two hours before his appointment?" Doc wondered.

"Good morning, Maggie."

"Good morning, Doc."

"I saw John in the car downstairs when I came in."

"Doc, he doesn't have to be here until 11:00 o'clock."

"I will ask him about this when I see him today."

After concluding an appointment with Mrs. Stinson, Doc walked into the waiting area and saw John sitting there with his eyes closed.

"Mr. Burton are you ready?"

"Yes." John was dressed in clean jeans, a red tank top shirt and blue flip-flops. He was clean shaven. He smelled slightly of a spicy cologne that Doc couldn't determine.

"John, please come back to my office so we can get started. How was your week?"

"Non-stop work."

"John, are you sleeping any better?"

"Yes, from exhaustion.

"How about your appetite?"

"About the same."

"John, when I came in this morning I noticed you were sitting in your car in the parking lot and it looked like you were in a deep sleep."

"Doc, I wanted to be here on time and I didn't want to be in the downtown shopping district with all of those people. I have had a good week and didn't want to ruin it by freaking out in traffic."

"John, it's not a problem. John, do you remember where we left off in the last session? You were telling me about running into your father."

"Oh yeah."

"John, what was it like growing up in your home before your dad left?"

"My Dad owned a plumbing contractor business in St. Louis on North Broadway and everyone knew him. We always had plenty of money and I was an only child. I didn't do too well at sports, especially football. I was only 5 feet 9 and weighed 145 pounds. My dad was 6 feet 4 and weighed 230 pounds and was built solid. I am sure that my size disappointed my father though he never said it directly. He would always hint and say things like, 'I hope you keep growing, John, and then maybe you can get on the varsity football team next year.' Dad criticized me continually while I was growing up, pointing out that my physical size wasn't adequate for football and my grades could be better even though I maintained a 4.0 average. Nothing I ever did was good enough for this man, even after I was awarded a full academic scholarship to Yale. Doc, I guess I grew up never feeling quite good enough. I allowed him to talk me out of going to Yale as he convinced me that I would be a failure there as well. He said the only thing that I could count on was a trade as a plumber, which he would teach me. It would always provide me with a good living."

"John, where was Mom in all of this?"

"Doc, as usual, she was ambivalent and didn't want me to leave the house. Mom had gotten so used to depending on me for most of her financial and emotional support after the old man walked out. I didn't have a life when I went to high school. I didn't have time for friends because I was too busy working at the grocery store, and the other free time I had was helping momma clean the house, go shopping, and then do my homework. I didn't have a date until I was 20 and I freaked out when she grabbed my hand at the movies. I ran outside and threw up in the alley. I was so embarrassed. The girl never knew and I could never bear to be around her after that."

"The only person I socialized with growing up, just like today, is myself. Doc, thanks."

"For what, John?"

"You are the first person in my life that I have ever told this story to. I have always been afraid of what others would say and how fast they would run away."

"John, you have spoken honestly about yourself today and that is pretty significant. Before we end today I want to discuss with you some homework assignments that will help you in therapy. I want you to write down three things that you identify as strengths and three things as accomplishments in your life. Please bring the list with you to your next session. I also want you to approach a stranger on the street and say 'Good morning' to them and wish them a good day."

"Doc, I can't do that!"

"John, please try. This will begin to improve your self-esteem. You already have begun the work necessary to decrease your acute sensitivity."

"How, Doc?"

"John, by talking honestly about yourself today and your feelings. It is a good start. John, have a great day and don't forget your homework assignments, and enjoy the beach. Please tell Maggie that you need an appointment in three weeks."

"John, can you see Doc at 2:00 p.m. in three weeks?" Maggie inquired.

"Sure."

It would be several months before John would call the office again and make another appointment. Another year had come and gone by now. It was New Years Eve, 2000 and the next day would begin 2001. The year 2000 felt like it just flew by. All Doc had to do now was get through all of the pyrotechnics and firecracker smoke and cover Mitzi's ears. She would go wild with the noise. Doc wondered if she didn't have an avoidant personality as well. Ha Ha, it was going to be a long night.

The noise was deafening and the smoke was almost suffocating. The smell of sulphur annoyed Mitzi as well and it seemed to linger in the air for nearly a week afterward.

As Doc exited the elevator he thought he noticed Mr. Burton going into the waiting room.

"I wonder if Maggie had scheduled him and forgot to tell me."

It had been months since Doc had last seen Mr. Burton. As he opened the door and walked into the waiting room, a loud voice boomed, "Doc!!!"

"Hello Mr. Burton, what a surprise to see you. It has been a while. Maggie, does Mr. Burton have an appointment?"

"No Doc, he doesn't."

There was no one in the waiting room yet, but Doc did not invite Mr. Burton to his office. Doc didn't want him to think he was willing to see him at that time.

"Mr. Burton, I can't see you today as I am booked solid and Maggie says everyone has confirmed. I remembered also that I had to meet some friends downtown at 7:00 at the concert hall." Doc never missed going to hear Beethoven's Ninth; it was like the best mental relaxation one could have. This year was going to be special, as the orchestra was going to have a full choir sing Schiller's Ode to Joy. Doc had third row floor seats and couldn't wait to see his friends. He hadn't been able to go out for a while due to the unexpected holiday demands on his calendar.

He noticed that Mr. Burton was very relaxed and well dressed.

"Doc, I understand. I was in the neighborhood and just got back into town and wanted to start up seeing you again. I hope you don't mind me dropping in to say hello and make an appointment."

"No not at all."

"Doc, I really trust you and know that you understand me."

"Maggie, put Mr. Burton on my calendar for next week."

"Is 4:00 p.m. all right, Mr. Burton?"

"Maggie, that will work for me." As Mr. Burton was leaving the office he approached Doc and handed him a sealed envelope. He said, "Doc this is for you. Please read it."

Doc slipped the envelope into his pocket.

It was a Sunday, the day Doc enjoyed greatly especially after an evening of listening to good music, eating good food, and spending quality time with good friends. He dressed and was on his way out the door for a morning jog, when out of his pants pocket dropped Mr. Burton's letter. Doc had forgotten all about it.

"I have fifteen minutes before I have to begin my one mile jog. I will have enough time to read it." Doc opened the envelope.

"To Doc: my social life consists of visiting internet chat rooms, where I exchange surface pleasantries with others in cyberspace, but I am careful never to reveal much about myself. I tell the people on the internet that my life is dull and ordinary, and there is little joy but they still want to get to know me and be my friend. I have thought about what you said about being avoidant. I remove myself from situations that would subject me to scrutiny as I have always done in my life. I realized after finding a self-help book on my own that I was behaving like an avoidant personality. When I first came to you, I was trying to change situations and change my personal circumstances so that I might bring myself more into the public eye. That is too frightening for me to do now and I don't feel like I am ready. The book I bought on my own talks about how people like me often times withdraw into their own private world of perceived inadequacies and self-doubts."

The letter went on, "Doc, I also went to a Christmas party that I know you would support me doing. My company hosted it and my boss highly encouraged me to attend, which I did with great reluctance. I froze when people asked me about my family and my background. My hands started to sweat and I felt like I wanted to run away but I didn't. I didn't feel that I was good enough for these people - they all were very successful people and very competent at handling social situations and interactions. I was afraid that if they knew about my family they would all laugh or run away from me. I have this preoccupation with being criticized or rejected in any social situation and this is a huge barrier that I know I have to overcome if I am going to be successful at building intimacy in any relationship. I remember the one step in the twelve-step mantra, 'One day at a time' as it continues to help me come in and out of recovery all of my life. I needed to get it right and this is the time to get it right."

"Doc, this is why I am choosing to come back into therapy with you. I trust you and you have helped me to start to identify my strengths and accomplishments. I did talk to two strangers on California Street outside of your office. The second person was easier to approach than the first. He smiled at me as I approached him. I think you referred to it as 'systematic desensitization' or did I read that in my self-help book? What does it matter - it makes sense and it works. Doc, I wrote enough and I am starting to get short of breath." John, Dec 21st 2001.

It had been a week since John dropped by the office and Doc was looking forward to discussing his letter with him at that day's appointment.

"Doc, Mr. Burton is here for his appointment."

"Thanks, Maggie can you bring his file back?"

"Mr. Burton please follow me. Doc will see you now. Doc, here is Mr. Burton's file.

"Thanks," Doc said as she closed the door. "Happy New Year, John," Doc intoned. "John, let me first start by saying that I am very impressed with the letter you wrote to me. It was honest and you even remembered your last homework assignment I gave you months ago about starting to identify your strengths and accomplishments. Oh, where have you been?"

"I flew to Oxford, England to see Walker and I stayed with him for several months. I started to crash after our last session. I knew what you were saying was true, but I just had to get away to clear my head. Doc, Walker says that you are the best. He also told me that I had to continue my journey and complete my therapy. I know he is right and I trust him like the brother I never had. I guess that makes you my Dad, Doc. Ha Ha." John then blurted out in a loud voice that surprised Doc, "Fix me Doc. You have all the answers, just tell me."

Doc knew from the updated intake form that Maggie had him fill out that nothing had changed in his life. He even had the same job. His employer held his job open for him because of his excellent skills as a plumber. John certainly had a good support system in place with his job and his close friendship with Walker.

"John, you are the only person who can fix you. You can access your answers if you just allow your mind to be open to living a new way, and use some of the tools and apply the skills you learn in your therapy. John, you reveal in your letter that you have been in and out of twelve-step programs most of your life. Where are you now?"

"I started a program at a church in the Mission District and we meet four times a week. I haven't drank for four months. Walker won't put up with it"

"Do you have a sponsor?"

"Yes," he stated with a smile on his face. "Doc, I stayed for the whole Christmas Party and I talked to two strangers on the street. I didn't feel like I wanted to throw up or I couldn't breathe. Doc, I have this fear of being rejected or ridiculed. When I am with a woman I become panicky. When I am on line I don't feel this way because I am anonymous and they can't get to me. Once I have sex with a woman, I want her to quit asking me to perform. I just want to hold her but I don't want to have to touch her anymore in that way. Doc, I am afraid to have interactions with women." John had a second life in cyberspace flirting with women he could keep at a distance and only touch on the computer screen that he stared at nightly.

"John, why are you afraid?"

"I just want to go to work and come home to myself. I will do something stupid or embarrassing and then I will be rejected. Then it will be just like it was with my father all over again," he said. Abruptly he added, "I guess our session is over, Doc."

"John yes, it is. I would like to see you next week to continue this conversation. I want you to bring in one accomplishment and one strength you have had in any relationship."

"Doc, I can do that now. I don't have any."

"I want you to go home and think about this. I am sure there is one strength and accomplishment you have had during one meaningful relationship."

"Give me an example Doc."

"Well, what about your relationship with Walker?"

"Oh, I see."

"Our session is over, and you should be very proud of yourself as you did some good work today and are really developing insight."

"Yea, I feel like I at least got an ear of the elephant eaten today," he said, laughing as he closed the office door.

John's fear of intimacy was overwhelming to him. He had to overcome this barrier if he was ever going to have an intimate relationship. Doc was perplexed with this client's intimacy fears, as he had never seen anyone with as much fear as John had. John was functioning marginally at work as well as struggling with the unresolved rejection he experienced at an early age by his selfish father and his emotionally unavailable mother. The challenge ahead was to continue to be consistent and build on the trust Doc had established with him. Doc also planned to provide him with some much-needed additional tools that would help John to start developing coping skills to manage these overwhelming scenarios in his life. Doc had a lot of work to do before John's next session. He made a note to explore more about his history of drinking at his next appointment.

John came to his next appointment on time, and Doc noticed he was carrying a huge journal notebook under his arm. Before Doc closed the door and sat down, John began to speak.

"Doc, I ain't nothing like my old man. He left my mother and treated me like hired help. Doc, I forgot to tell you something else last week. I am a recovering alcoholic and have been sober for three months and attend Alcoholics Anonymous weekly, but I can never stand up in front of the crowd and speak. I just sit way in the back all by myself and listen. I really like the church. It is in the Mission District, and I have a great guy named Harry as my sponsor. He tells me that when I am ready, I can stand up and tell them 'My name is John and I am an alcoholic.' He says that therapy saved his life and helped him. He told me he is glad that I am seeing someone. I trust him also."

"John, tell me a little about your drinking history."

"Well Doc, I have drunk everything from imported scotch to cheap cologne. I have eaten out of trashcans and have slept on the streets. I started drinking with my father once I finished the vocational school that I transferred to after I gave up my scholarship to Yale. I apprenticed with him after that for four years. He always told me if I work hard then I should drink hard. I started to have a lot of blood in my stool and I was hospitalized for the first time when I was 37. The bleeding stopped and I left the hospital and continued to drink. The fourth time I was hospitalized for internal bleeding an internist told me I was an alcoholic and I had to quit drinking or I wouldn't make it to my 40th birthday. They finally had my attention."

"John, I would like to know how long you have been off of the streets? How did you get sober?"

"Doc, I have been off of the streets for a couple of years, and I quit drinking when I was released two years ago from my last rehab center. I decided then that I could and wanted to quit drinking. I have been in and out of rehab and gamed all of the treatment professionals until I met you. I knew you were the one that could help me. I knew I could use the system as a respite from the streets as some bleeding heart would feel sorry for me and continue to let me be re-cycled, but no one ever gave me what I needed. I was known as the Rehab Frequent Flyer, and I had more miles than anyone."

"What is it you think you needed, John?"

"I don't know Doc; you have all of the answers. You tell me."

"John do you think you are avoiding taking responsibility for yourself?"

"Yes, I do."

"John, how long do you remember your dad drinking?"

"All I remember is that he drank as long as I can remember, and he drank like a fish and then he would beat the hell out of me and my mother and then laugh at us. I hate this man!"

"Did anyone know what was going on in your house in the community?"

"No you didn't talk about personal stuff like this to other people."

"John, is your father still alive?"

"No the old bastard is dead!"

"How about your mother?"

"No she is in heaven away from all of her pain. Doc, I don't want to talk about him. Is our session about over? I have to go home."

Doc had pushed a button that made him feel anxious.

"John, I will see you next week. We need to get back to talk about one of your strengths and accomplishments in a relationship."

"Oh yeah. I forgot we kind of got sidetracked." John hesitated and asked, "Doc, how long do you think this will take?"

"John, this problem did not get here over night and it won't be fixed over night. You have to trust in the process."

During preparation for John's next therapy session, Doc planned to convey to John that when we become involved with another individual, there are really no guarantees whether or not we will be liked and accepted. But for John, the risk of becoming involved with anyone without an ironclad guarantee of being liked and accepted was nearly impossible to endure.

As John sat down on the couch he blurted out, "Doc, why can't I be normal?"

"John, what do you think 'normal' means?"

"Someone who isn't like me."

"John, what is wrong with someone like you?"

"People run away from me once they know about me."

"John, isn't it you who are running away from others?"

John was speechless for the first time since he came to see Doc. "How do you know this stuff about me, Doc?"

"Are you saying you agree?"

"Yes," he said softly.

"John, can we begin where we left off last week?"

"Do we have to talk about my father?"

"John, have you made peace with your father?"

"Doc, I have nothing to resolve."

"Then why do you still hate him?"

There was a deafening silence in the room. John asked, "How does not making peace with my father keep me from being intimate?"

"John, you have to acknowledge and release these feelings toward your father if you want to be free to love and grow. We can't change yesterday, but we can affect what happens in our lives from this moment forward. John, the feelings you have towards your father are blocking your growth."

"How do I resolve my feelings, Doc?"

"Give me one strength and accomplishment about a relationship you've had or are now in."

"All right, Doc. I trust you, and that is a strength. I feel that I am understanding myself more by coming to see you, and that is an accomplishment."

"John, I knew you could do it. John, you have to accept the reality that your father was incapable of having any healthy relationship. He could never show love, as he probably didn't understand it himself."

"Doc, he told me once his uncle had molested him and he never trusted anyone again in his life."

"John, let us pretend your father is sitting in this chair. Tell him how you feel."

"I can't, Doc."

"Why?"

"I am scared."

"What are you are afraid of John?"

"That he will hurt me again."

"John, he can't hurt you ever again."

The next thing Doc knew John was screaming, "Why did you hurt us? Didn't you know we loved you and only wanted your approval? But you never could say one nice thing to anyone! Whatever I did wasn't good enough for you. I was never the man you wanted me to be. God, I hate you!!!" He then started to weep uncontrollably and finally blurted out, "Damn that felt good!"

"John, that is enough for today. I want you to think about what happened today and write your thoughts down in your journal and bring to your next session."

Doc thought John was clueless at this time how much he had accomplished. Time would reveal this to him, and his insight would continue to be fine-tuned.

"Thanks Doc, and may you have a great weekend," he said as he skipped out the door. "I will see you in two weeks."

John missed the next appointment due to an emergency but assured Doc he would make the next one scheduled. It had been 6 weeks since the last session with John, and Doc wondered how he was doing.

When Doc thought about John's personal history, he was reminded of the great wisdom of Buddha. He spoke volumes about where John had been, where he currently was in his life and where he was going in his life in the quote,

"Do not pursue the past.
Do not lose yourself in the future.
The past no longer is.
The future has not yet come.
Looking deeply at life as it is
In the very here and now,
The practitioner dwells
In stability and freedom.

We must be diligent today.
To wait until tomorrow is too late"

John was on time for the next appointment that he had scheduled with Maggie. Before Doc said anything, John blurted, "Doc I met someone on the internet and she wants to get to know me. I sent her a $1,000 airline ticket to fly to San Francisco to spend time with me. I am panicked now. I don't want her to come, but I can't cancel her flight. It is too late."

"John, do you think you acted impulsively?"

"Yes, and I am foolish." John spluttered, "Doc, what do I do now? I feel like such a loser. I know I have disappointed you."

"John, you have not disappointed me. Let's talk about this. Do you know why you did this?"

"Yes."

"John, could you please tell me?"

"This girl sounded really sincere on the internet and said she really wanted to get to know me, and she also was looking for a relationship. I am so lonely and desperate for a relationship."

"John do you think you are healthy enough for a relationship now?"

"No I guess not."

"I want you to have a good relationship with someone who is healthy when you are healthier."

"I asked her if she would fly here to see me and she said she would if I sent her an airline ticket. I went out the next day and paid for it."

"Have you talked to the girl since you bought the ticket?"

"Yes, and she is so excited to be coming to San Francisco."

"John, where is she from?"

"Arkansas I think, or is it Oklahoma? Doc, she has never been out of the town she lives in, much less ever flown on an airplane."

"John, do you hear what you just told me?"

"Yeah, it doesn't sound like I was too aware of anything going on around me and she doesn't sound too healthy, either."

"John, ask yourself this question. If I were a woman, why would I fly 1000 plus miles to meet a complete stranger?"

"Doc, no emotionally healthy woman would."

"Precisely, John. I think it took a lot of courage for you to put yourself out there like this. I want to give you positive feedback and reinforce your efforts even though they were a little amiss. I don't think you are ready for an intimate relationship yet. You are still working on understanding what healthy versus unhealthy looks like. I think you should continue the work you started to get healthy and you will eventually meet the right woman, but you still have some work to do in therapy. John, you need to continue working on improving your self-esteem and continue journaling to identify goals for desired changes, and you need to break them down into manageable steps for shaping new behavior. Are you still maintaining sobriety?"

"Yes, and I have an AA meeting tonight at the church. I realized that I don't need any chemicals to make me be happy. Since I started coming to therapy, I even look at sunsets differently and appreciate them in a totally different way."

As the session ended, Doc knew that John was well on his way toward stepping onto the road leading eventually to his long elusive recovery. It would take some time before he was ready for the relationship that he so desperately desired. Doc believed he would wait, and would know when it was the right time and that he had met the right person.

"Doc, I am going to see Walker next month in Paris and we are going to do some sightseeing. I can't wait to tell him all of the stuff I have learned from you. I am glad I saved some extra money. My employer told me to go ahead, and that he would keep my job open until I came back. I want to see more of the world with a clear head and sober. Can I see you when I get back?"

"Of course. Just keep journaling and attending AA, and don't forget to talk to strangers. Good luck and safe journey."

Doc never heard from John and never knew if he made it to Paris. Walker had quit e-mailing progress reports to the office a month prior to John's last appointment. Doc hoped that John would stay on his path to recovery, and continue to eat his elephant one bite at a time. He was sure that John only had a little left on his plate to eat.

Susan Saver

Doc was on the way out of town to attend a conference, struggling to drag a set of over-packed suitcases through the airport. He boarded his flight, and as he flew all night, Doc noticed many people struggling throughout the flight. They pulled their bags down from the overhead compartments, got a few things out of the bags, and then pushed the bags back in their overhead compartments. It seemed that the passengers who struggled the most throughout the flight and appeared the most anxious were the ones who brought the largest bags, bags that were cumbersome to carry and that barely fit in the overhead compartments. Rather than prepare a smaller bag that contained in-flight necessities, the owners of these big bags stuffed them full, then proceeded to pull them down and go through them throughout the duration of the flight in order to find a book, a pillow, or a snack. They would allow their bags to hit other passengers in the process, or the bag would fall on another passenger, annoying them and disrupting the flight. The passengers who came equipped with small bags were not as annoying or disruptive as the ones that brought the big bags. They did not incessantly go through their bags to find snacks or a book to read during the flight.

"Doc, can I get you anything?" the sky hostess asked.

"No thanks." It was 11:00 p.m. and Doc still had four more hours of flying time left before he landed in Honolulu. He was glad that he was finally flying back home. He had enjoyed the conference in Dallas, but was excited to get home to his family. In just a couple of months it would be the year 2003, and then the neighborhood kids would be at Doc's house wanting candy for Halloween again. It seems that Halloween had just occurred, and it was still 2001. Time was just flying by.

Doc couldn't believe that it had only been six months since he had sold the practice to Maggie after she graduated and got her clinical license. Doc wanted to work with soldiers and their families and had settled down in Hawaii, as there was a large population of military families living there. Doc couldn't believe how much he had settled in after being there just under a year. "I guess this is where I need to be at this moment," Doc thought.

A fact of life we all face as we get older is that time does fly by. It really doesn't go by any faster, it just seems that way. Doc dozed off during his flight, and the next thing he heard was the Captain's voice on the intercom advising, "Please fasten your seat belts. We will be landing at Honolulu International Airport in ten minutes."

Doc struggled to get his luggage, which incidentally, did not contain any more unresolved issues and emotions. (Doc had unpacked most of those bags shortly after he arrived in San Francisco years ago. That was all behind him now). Doc recalled how his past struggle had been like those of his clients, dealing with their (emotional) baggage. Unknown to him at the time was how significant this metaphor would become as a therapeutic tool. Doc would help clients visualize their own emotional struggles with the baggage that they carried in their lives. This metaphor would be a powerful mechanism, helping them to visualize their need to work through issues. Doc also used the metaphor to motivate clients to begin the hard work of unpacking and managing their emotional bags. He wondered what clients would think if one of them happened to see him strain under the weight of his own baggage during deplaning. Doc wondered if they would see the irony of his situation.

Problems and drama unfold for people who carry emotional baggage, and they inadvertently impose both on those around them. The baggage they carry seems to rule their lives. A cognizant awareness and empathy of others' struggles can offer insight on how to manage emotional baggage. How much we carry around with us helps to determine the length and the quality of our journey through our lives. Helping clients identify and take responsibility for their own baggage and not volunteer to carry someone else's around had proven to be a successful therapeutic technique that has had resounding success for many of Doc's clients.

As the plane landed, everyone jumped to their feet and started to deplane. Doc noticed that the passengers who had small bags had them out of the overhead compartments before anyone started to deplane. On the other hand, the passengers with the big bags fought to pry them loose from the overhead compartments where they had jammed them in at the beginning of the flight. The passengers struggling with large bags interrupted the steady flow of passengers carrying smaller bags deplaning. It was like observing a traffic jam on a plane. It was a 200-passenger pile up. If a passenger had to catch a connecting flight that had small bags and was under a time constraint, they were just out of luck unless they happened to have access to the emergency exits, or were personally escorted off of the plane by a sky host/hostess.

The entire flight experience reminded Doc of one of his clients' lives, and he recalled her story on his drive home from the airport. Doc had met Susan Saver at a charity function in January, 2003 where she was raising money so that soldiers and their families could attend weekend retreats offering the emotional ballast to help with the consequences of numerous deployments. Susan was in her late 30s, was overweight, and had long red hair. Her piercing blue eyes were beautiful, but appeared to continually express sadness, and were always watering as if she were preparing to cry. Susan appeared depressed and anxious throughout the fifteen minutes during which Doc introduced himself and briefly spoke with her and her husband, Tim. She appeared disheveled but clean. Her hair was arranged in a way that made it look like she had put her finger in a light socket before the party. She appeared to have a great command of social and military etiquette, and also was adept and skilled at conversing fluently about art and literature, drawing upon a vast array of knowledge.

"Doc," she began, "My husband is a Colonel, and we have been married for over seven years. We have no children and this is a first marriage for both of us." She paced back and forth, her eyes watering. She held her head down, and did not look very happy. Doc had no idea why Susan began her conversation with him in this way, as it had not been solicited by anyone that he was aware of. He found this impulsive behavior to be alarming, and his clinical mind was starting to take over. He had to remind himself that he was not here as a clinician but as a guest and nothing more.

Susan couldn't stop talking about her life with Tim and the fifteen minutes she spent with Doc made him feel as though he had administered an hour long session of therapy.

"Doc, I do not work but I am always busy putting on dinner parties for the generals and other high-ranking senior leaders at Tim's insistence." Doc discovered later that Susan secretly sought an escape route out of this marriage. Telling Tim was an option she could never use with Tim. When he wanted something for himself he was heedless as to anything she said or felt.

Tim was in his late 30s and successful in his career, but his behavior appeared to be a little negative and guarded. Doc also noticed that his facial expression was tense throughout the time he spent in his presence. He was very well groomed, and like Susan, he seemed to be knowledgeable in an array of topics and very adept at military etiquette and protocol. He was immaculate in his dress uniform; there wasn't a wrinkle anywhere on the uniform and the brass buttons shone when the sun hit them.

"Tim," Susan softly said, "I want you to meet Doc. He says he is a therapist and helps couples."

"Susan we don't have any trouble in our marriage," Tim countered, nervously laughing as he shook Doc's hand.

"Tim, how do you get your uniform so perfectly ironed?"

"Susan stays up all night ironing and starching it until it is just perfect. She knows I get angry if there is one wrinkle in the pant leg or on the jacket. Susan is like my mother. She takes care of me, and I know she loves doing it. That is why she chose to marry me. We both don't want or have any time for children. We barely have time enough for each other," he said, laughing. I noticed Susan held her head down the whole time Tim spoke as if embarrassed by what he was saying.

Doc looked at his watch, and knew he had to go. His Ohana (the Hawaiian word for family, both blood and non-blood related) expected him home for dinner. He said his good byes to Susan and Tim, and thanked them both for sponsoring the fund raiser.

"Susan, the food was delicious. You certainly are a good cook."

"Doc, you are too kind. Please let me walk you to your car." As Susan and Doc walked towards the car, Susan quietly whispered that she would like to have Doc's business card. Doc asked her why she was speaking so softly and she replied that she didn't want Tim to hear or know that she was thinking about seeing a therapist. "He would be angry and yell at me for hours," she hissed. "Tim believes that what we do in our home stays in our home and no one needs to know about any of our problems, especially a therapist."

"Susan, here is my card. If you would like to see me call Lani for an appointment." Driving away from the base, Doc ruminated on his impressions of Tim and Susan. They definitely seemed to be having issues of control in their marriage. Doc was to find out later that their marriage was indeed very dysfunctional and broken. Doc had a momentary flash regarding the metaphor of baggage (emotional) he used with clients from his earlier plane ride.

Doc knew Susan was reaching out and possibly was seeking an escape route, but he didn't know if she would ever quite make it to the door. Doc imagined that if Susan had been on his flight, no one could have been able to deplane for quite a while until Susan dragged her baggage down the aisle and exited.

Doc got home and found himself exhausted. He gave all of his family quick kisses good night and excused himself. Once his head hit the pillow, he fell fast asleep, thinking, "There's no place like home ... there's no place like home."

Lani Rodrigo was great in the office but unlike Maggie, she had no aspirations to become a clinician herself. She was content coming in, doing quality work, and then spending time with her family and friends on the weekends. Her agenda sometimes included either the beach or the mountains for some good hiking. Lani was striking, with waist-length, raven black hair and exotic almond eyes. She was in her mid 30's, single, and was 5'1." She attended the university part-time and was studying architecture, and shared a condo with other graduate students in Manoa. Although not supermodel thin, her weight was proportional to her height, and she was very proud of her Portuguese father and Hawaiian mother. Clients loved her as she could "talk story" (a Hawaiian colloquialism for informal conversations) with any of them, but she was always very professional. They do things differently in the islands than in the midwest, and Doc believed that his understanding of the term "talk story" was another indication that he was settling in to his new home quite nicely after being there only for a short period of time.

Doc decorated the office by himself. Lani said she didn't know anything about colors or what would look good together. Doc missed Maggie, but he had learned a lot from her about furniture styles and colors. He had picked up a mocha leather wingback chair and a 90" couch at the flea market in Aiea. He added a tropical flavor to the office by bringing in a banana tree and some coffee plants. They did great with the amount of sunlight that came into the office throughout the day. The walls were painted a pearl grey.

Doc's office was also in a great location, overlooking Pearl Harbor. Clients sometimes would comment that they couldn't cry in the office as it was too beautiful when they looked out on the water watching the clouds roll by. The view included the USS Arizona Memorial, USS Missouri and periodically clients caught a glimpse of the beautiful colors that hit the hills of Makakilo as the sun set for the day.

Doc shared a large waiting room – with three other therapists that had an adequate reception station in front of the offices where Lani sat. Doc's office was approximately fifty feet to the left of the reception station. Unlike the office in San Francisco, there was no hallway to go down or back exit for clients. The physical layout was appropriate, but Doc had to make sure Lani was always aware of this when she scheduled clients, in order to minimize the opportunity for clients to run into each other, clients who might be acquainted either personally or professionally. The office environment needed to make clients feel safe. The new office was bigger than the one in San Francisco, and offered Doc greater flexibility to host group, family, or individual therapy sessions. It was definitely a much bigger office than he was used to.

Doc met with Susan a week after their initial meeting at her request for individual therapy. As Lani escorted Susan down to the office, Doc was struck by her appearance and lack of grooming as she sat down on the sofa. Her hair was all matted and she looked even more disheveled than she had at their first meeting. Her clothes were very wrinkled and they emitted a pungent odor. Her makeup was poorly applied. Her lipstick had smeared across her chin, her eyeliner was all over her upper cheekbone and she was malodorous.

"Doc, I am unhappy and tired of taking care of Tim. I miss not having any children."

"Susan before we start talking about that let me get some information on your family of origin."

What do you want to know?"

"Susan tell me about your mother and the rest of your family."

"Doc, first thing I want to say is my mother pulled on my hair and always told me to act pretty when I was around men, especially my father. Tim pulls on my hair sometimes to get my attention and it makes me very angry. Mom would insist that I look pretty for my father whenever he would return from being gone just like Tim wants me to look pretty when he comes back from his deployment."

"My father was never available for my needs as he was in the military service and was always traveling with deployments and was gone often for many months at a time. Mom would stay in bed for days feeling depressed while Dad was gone and she would drink and cry in her room. As a child I often got myself off to school on my own as Mom was often too sick to prepare me for school and Dad was gone often."

"Susan, do you feel you have been abandoned most of your life?"

"Doc, I have always felt alone and I try hard to make my husband happy and proud of me."

It appeared that Susan could be hurt easily and tried very hard to please others, often at her own emotional expense.

"Susan, tell me why you and Tim don't have any children."

"Tim wanted me to take care of him and didn't want to share me with any children we may have. I went along with this. I didn't want to disappoint him. He is, after all, my husband and that is what a good wife should do. My father left my mother because she wanted children and he didn't. I was devastated by that."

"Who told you that, Susan?"

"My mom told me because my father wanted no children that I was a mistake. She yells at me that I should want what Tim does and warns me that what happened to her might happen to me. Because of the grief I caused my parents, I didn't want to have children with Tim and cause undue grief in our marriage."

Susan's speech was pressured, she sat slouched over and she appeared to be very restless because she rubbed her forearms continually throughout the session. Susan seemed to be in a great deal of stress.

"Susan, I want to teach you a breathing technique now that will help you relax."

"Okay, Doc." Susan had become agitated after telling me the details of her childhood and her relationship with Tim. Doc redirected her and got her to refocus and relax first before she went any further.

After practicing focused breathing, Susan remarked, "Doc I can't believe how that breathing technique got rid of the migraine that I had when I came in. I get a lot of them. I also can't lose any weight. Tim yells and screams at me all of the time to lose weight."

The session came to a close.

"Susan, I want you to start journaling your thoughts daily, and to write whatever comes to mind in the morning about the preceding day. Please bring your journal to your next session. Journaling is a tool that can be used to help you develop better coping skills that will help you manage the daily stressors in your life. By recording your thoughts daily, you have a record of how you are handling things. It is like a daily report card of your progress and it helps you move towards getting better. Susan, do you understand now why it is so important for you to journal?"

"Yea, Doc," she softly said, her head down and her eyes gazing toward the floor.

Doc suspected that there was a lot more to Susan's story than was disclosed at her first appointment. He was to find out that his suspicions were correct.

A week had gone by since Susan's initial appointment. Doc eagerly awaited the second session with Susan scheduled for 10:00 a.m. He wanted to gather more information about her life, so that he could piece together more of her puzzling story and to assess how well she managed her stress during the week.

Doc showed his 9:00 a.m. appointment out of the office and went to get Susan. She wasn't in the waiting room.

"One more week and Lani will be back from her vacation on the mainland," Doc sighed. He couldn't wait to see her smiling face again. He was getting tired of running a one-man show. It brought back memories of the stressful days with no help in the San Francisco office, and he knew he didn't want to have a repeat performance. Doc double checked his daytimer and verified that Susan did indeed have her second appointment that day at 10:00 a.m.

He assumed she must be running late, or was caught in traffic. The next time Doc looked at his watch, it was 10:30 and still Susan had not arrived. He knew at that point if she did come in, her appointment would be cut short to thirty minutes, as Doc already had another client booked for 11:00 and he was already in the waiting room.

At 10:45 a.m. Susan showed up in the office crying. Her body was trembling and her appearance was as haphazard as it was the last time I saw her. She still reeked, she wore no makeup, and her hair was matted and appeared to be unwashed. Doc had no idea that this was how her appearance and behavior was most of the time, unless she was being the perfect wife and hostess for Tim.

Susan appeared to be in a crisis mode by her behaviors. Doc was unclear as to what Susan's expectations from therapy were at this point. Susan, like so many others carrying big bags of emotions, had no problem dropping them on others, making others uncomfortable, and delaying everyone's progress including her own. Susan didn't have any boundaries and Doc believed he needed to model some for her.

"Susan, before we get started I want to address a concern I have. You are late for your appointment today and we only have fifteen minutes today to work."

"Doc, I am sorry. I will try and be brief."

"Susan did you understand what I said?"

"Yea, and I said I was sorry. It won't happen again, okay?" she snapped back. "Doc, I think I am being emotionally and verbally abused by Tim."

"Do you fear for your safety, Susan?"

"No, Doc he has never hit me but I think I am being abused."

"Let's explore this further, Susan. Do you know the difference between physical, emotional, verbal, and sexual abuse?"

"Yes, and from what I have been reading on the Internet, I think I am being abused verbally and emotionally by Tim and I want it to stop. He says he loves me in the morning and I do something he doesn't like then he calls me fat and ugly. I get so confused."

"Susan, unlike most victims of spousal abuse, you are acknowledging and admitting that abuse has and is still occurring. That is a big step towards recovery."

"Doc, it exists in my marriage and has been going on for seven years, and still is. I have been in denial about it. I am so afraid he will leave and I will be all alone with nothing." Susan's eyes watered and this time she wept uncontrollably for a couple of minutes. "What do I do now Doc?"

Doc knew that Susan could be receptive to therapy that was focused, but he had to teach her how she could make the necessary changes needed in her life. He was only going to hear Susan's side of the story, as Tim refused to come into therapy to work on the marriage, even after several requests from Susan.

Because Susan was the one who had sought individual therapy, Doc tried his best to give her tools and help teach her skills that could help her to begin to elevate her low self-esteem. Susan had to lay the role of caretaker aside in her marriage and start to deal with her fears and her abuse. She had fears but she had not spoken of them out loud until today. She had to first take responsibility for her own life. Susan had to change the way she thought and she had to begin to discern and be more perceptive to things happening in her life. This would help her immensely with the development of healthier decision making processes.

Doc used an attention getting statement with Susan that he had heard from a friend long ago in graduate school.

"Susan, people need to get rid of their stinking thinking if they ever want to get better. Over the years, using discernment and perception has enabled me to assist clients with them fixing themselves, which only they have the power to do."

Susan's worldview of her marriage was skewed, as she continually coped and faced Tim's abuse by staying out of his way and making sure she did nothing that would upset him. Her coping mechanism had been denial until she walked into Doc's office, and realized that she could no longer avoid or deny the dysfunction in her marriage.

Doc continued to explain, "Susan, victims of spousal abuse are beaten down emotionally, suffer from low self-esteem, have feelings of worthlessness or unworthiness, and are convinced that they are incapable of managing their own lives and often feel out of control in their lives. This describes a situation very much like yours. Susan, our fifteen minutes went by fast and I will see you in a week."

"Thanks Doc, I feel a little better than when I came in. I am sorry I was late. I will be on time next time."

"Susan, one final thought. The major problem you have with your partner is that Tim doesn't speak the same language as you do. One of your goals in therapy is going to be for you to learn to develop these skills so that his language can be understood. If Tim doesn't want to change or go into therapy as well, you are going to have a one-sided conversation."

"Thanks Doc, for the advice."

It is imperative to convey to clients that their discernment and perception are their partners, and both want only to guide them. They need to listen.

Susan came in for her third appointment on time. Doc noticed that she wore a lot of makeup, her clothes were neatly pressed, her hair was clean and there was a freshly showered smell about her. Even her nails appeared to be manicured. This was not the same person who appeared at the last two meetings.

"Susan, how are you today?"

"Doc, I couldn't be better."

She kept looking at her watch and fidgeted as the minutes ticked by.

"Susan, do you need to reschedule your session?"

"No, but I have to leave on the hour as Tim expects me home to clean the house and cook dinner for thirty people tonight." Susan whimpered, "I'll be up all night cleaning up."

"Susan how is Tim?"

"He is at home waiting for me, just waiting to have a reason to yell and scream and call me fat and ugly."

"Susan, you need to tell Tim to quit calling you fat and ugly when you get home today. Tell him that you do not like that, and not to ever call you that again. Do you understand Susan? You have to set a boundary with Tim, or he will continue to verbally and emotionally abuse you. Susan, you have to set the boundary!"

"I will try," Susan moaned.

"Did you bring your journal?"

"No, I have forgotten all about doing the journaling assignment. I don't have the time anyway."

"Susan, you really need to begin journaling as it will help you begin to think differently and change the way you react to stressors."

Doc started to become concerned. He had already seen her now three times, and had not noticed anything getting better for her except her appearance at this session. He suspected the change was at Tim's request, not because Susan wanted to do it. Her self-esteem was still very low, and Doc didn't know how long she could continue with this level of anxiety before crashing.

"Susan, how have you been sleeping and eating?"

"Doc, I haven't," she stammered, with tears streaming down her face. "I also am having diarrhea and can't keep anything down."

"Susan, do you think any of the emotional stress you have been dealing with can affect your physical health?"

"No," she said abruptly, "but if it is medical I might not have to come and see you anymore Doc. Tim might love me even more if I quit coming here. You know he doesn't believe in what you do, and doesn't think you or anyone in your field can help anyone, especially me."

"Susan, why do you continue to come and see me if you aren't going to do the homework I assign?"

"Doc, I like talking to you. Isn't that enough?"

"Susan, it is not enough. I need to set some guidelines for you. Thanks for being on time today, but you must bring your journal in next time you see me or we can't continue therapy."

"Ok, Doc," Susan said softly.

"Susan, I am concerned and want you to see your medical doctor as soon as possible so that we can rule out any physical reasons for your symptoms. I want you to call me as soon as you have the results of your exam."

"Doc, I have to go. I will call you next week to schedule another appointment and let you know my results from the exam. I really have to go," Susan said as she paced back and forth in the office, "or Tim will be upset if I don't get that party prepared for all of the military brass."

Susan relaxed a little, knowing there was a possibility that her symptoms could be a result of an imbalance in her body and nothing more. Susan was still in denial and had been unable to see how her current emotional state could possibly be affecting her physical health. Doc believed that her medical doctor would be able to assess this and communicate this to her. Doc hoped that she would follow up on his recommendation to see her medical doctor and not let Tim talk her out of it.

Doc was going through his appointment book and realized that it was almost Easter. He also noticed that Susan had not called in with the results of her medical exam, nor had she scheduled another appointment even though it had been well over three weeks since her last session. Doc pulled her medical record and dialed the phone. It rang three times and then went to voice mail.

"Susan, this is Doc. Please call me as soon as you can."

Within one minute, Doc's phone rang.

"Hello?"

"Doc this is Susan. I got your message and need to see you as soon as possible."

"Susan, I have a cancellation today at 4:00 p.m. Can you make that appointment?"

"Doc, I will be there at 4:00 p.m. I can't wait to see you."

Susan was pacing anxiously in the waiting room and kept looking at her watch as she had done at the last appointment.

"Susan, are you ready?"

"Yes, Doc."

"Susan, how have you been?"

"Fine," she said. "Doc, how have you been?"

"Fine as well, Susan. Did you bring the results of your medical exam and your journal?"

Susan turned quiet and lowered her head. She said softly, "I am sorry."

"Susan, what are you sorry for?"

"I forgot, Doc. I never went for the exam, because Tim forbade me to go. He said I was just pretending to be sick so I could get his attention."

"Susan, why did you come and see me today? You haven't followed my recommendations so far."

"Doc, I like talking to you, and I feel safe in here."

Doc supposed the reason for Susan's resistance to any of his recommendations was that she refused to see herself being anything other than Tim's caretaker/wife. She had become numb to his abuse over the years. In her mind, it was normal, and it now was her new emotional baseline.

"Doc, are you angry at me?"

"Susan, I am not mad at you." Doc hesitated, then asked, "What do you want out of life?"

Susan was quiet for at least ten minutes and with eyes watering shouted, "I want out of this lousy marriage." Susan then smiled and asked, "Where were we?" Doc sensed she was frustrated and maybe in a state of despair by her outburst.

"Susan, therapy does not tell you what to do, but teaches you to decide for yourself and to make decisions for yourself. Do you understand that?"

"Yes," she softly stated.

"Susan, I have given you numerous homework assignments that are important factors in your therapy, but you refuse to do them. These homework assignments are important as they will help you to practice the techniques you learn in therapy to cope with the stressors of your life situation and make the changes you need to make. That is, if you are serious about choosing an emotionally healthier way in which to live."

Susan nodded in agreement. "Doc, I understand how important therapy and the homework is for me to do in order to begin to understand why I need to change. I know I will change once I accept the need to change my situation. Doc, I will come prepared for the next session."

Doc thought, "I hope this was just not another attempt to placate me." He continued with Susan, "You must still go to your medical doctor before our next appointment as I requested you do in our last session, so we can rule out any medical problems. Call me on the phone and have your physician fax me over the results before your next appointment."

"I will, and I will come prepared for the next session."

As the session continued Doc asked Susan, "Have you done any journaling?"

"No, I forgot to bring the journal and I haven't written anything in it."

"Susan, for your homework assignment I want you to write in your journal daily in the morning about the preceding day. I want you to write about any unwanted feelings and behaviors you are experiencing. I also want you to try and identify what the cause of these feelings and behaviors are. I want you to write a definition of what you think a boundary is. I want you to list the boundaries that you think exist in your marriage. Susan we are going to focus your therapy on learning how to replace negative thoughts with thoughts that would lead to more desirable reactions and an understanding of the importance of boundaries in any and all relationships."

Susan's demeanor abruptly changed from someone who was actively listening to someone who was acting fearful and anxious to leave my office.

"Doc, this all makes a lot of sense but I have to go. Tim will be upset if I am late."

"Susan, you need to focus on the area of boundaries and your negative thoughts before our next appointment."

"Doc, I really have to go now. See you next week and yeah, I will call you after I see my medical doctor for my exam." On her way out, she dropped her journal. Doc thought this interesting, since she had said she hadn't done the journal. He made a mental note to discuss this at the next appointment.

Her journal opened when it fell. Doc picked it up and noticed writing on many of the pages; the book was at least a half-inch thick. Doc mused, "Had Susan really forgotten or had she planned to drop this off after she left?" It appeared that Susan actually was writing in her journal and she came to therapy. Her coming to therapy and dropping her journal was indicating a lessening of resistance by Susan. She also continually chose not to reveal any of her innermost thoughts to Doc in her sessions but chose to jot them down in the journal that she wanted Doc to read. Doc surmised that she might have wanted him to pick up the journal and read her thoughts in her absence. He deduced that this might be a way for her to communicate without betraying Tim. None of her innermost thoughts had been revealed at any of the therapy sessions to date, so she never had to feel that anything she had spoken of was a betrayal.

Doc also surmised that Susan may have thought that by dropping the journal, she might have an out. If she lost her journal, then she would be exempt from writing anything else down in it.

Issues related to Susan's motivation had to be observed over time. Her stated reasons for entering treatment varied. Susan wasn't presenting for treatment out of her own personal desire for change. It was rather a response to an external demand, and that external demand was named Tim. Doc placed Susan's unread journal in her file and made a note in her chart to ask her to read it out loud to him at her next appointment.

Doc finally received a call from Susan after several weeks of silence. It came on a Saturday, and Susan was crying uncontrollably.

"Doc, I feel like harming myself."

"Susan, I am going to call 911 and I want you to stay on the phone talking to me." As Doc dialed 911, he heard Susan's breathing becoming labored.

Doc knew he had to stall for time and keep her on the telephone until the ambulance could get to her house. At this point, Susan gave a hundred excuses why she couldn't go to the emergency room.

"Doc, I can't go to the hospital. I have to mop the floors and cook for another party of twenty five on Sunday that Tim is having over at our house. Doc, he has folks coming in from the Pentagon, and everything he has worked for in his career is riding on this dinner. I can't screw it up or it will be the end of us. He told me so tonight."

"Susan, I want you to take care of yourself and I am making the decision for you in this situation. I want you to keep talking to me." Doc knew that Emergency Medical Services would be there in a short period of time.

"Doc, there is someone knocking at the door ... can you hold on?"

"Sure," Doc answered. He was hoping it was EMS. The next thing he heard was a male voice on the other end saying, "This is Mr. Turner from Emergency Medical Services. We are going to stabilize Mrs. Saver first and then take her right to the hospital."

Susan was not hospitalized and was released to her husband within eight hours of being evaluated at the Emergency Room. The attending physician was an intern who had deemed her as not being a threat to herself or to others. This unparalleled opportunity for Susan to get medical attention was just lost. Doc vowed to keep trying to reach her.

Susan called Doc on Monday. She was laughing and kept repeating that she was happy.

"Doc, Tim is taking me to Mexico for a much needed vacation. We are getting along so much better now. Doc, I realized that when I take care of Tim and do these dinner parties at his request, then I feel better about myself. Tim says all I have to do is this last dinner party and he is sure to get his promotion. After Tim gets his promotion he says everything will be the way it used to be when we first got married."

Doc was even more concerned for Susan. He recognized that she was in the "honeymoon phase" of the abuse.

"Doc, Tim has apologized for everything and says he loves me and promises to change his yelling and says he won't call me fat or ugly anymore. Tim is even willing to come and see you. What do you think about that? Doc, are you still there?"

Doc paused to figure what he needed to say to convince her that she was just in another phase of the abuse and it was the final stage.

Susan had been reaching out in her own way, but she did not know how to accept the help that was being offered. Doc always wanted Susan to be committed to do the hard work necessary to change her life, and to sincerely want her life to change. A therapist can only hope that when a client comes in the door, they want to make changes to improve their life. Unfortunately, the client sometimes decides they prefer the familiarity of their current situation to facing the fears that come from the unknowns related to change. Doc was afraid that was the plateau where Susan found herself.

Doc always emphasized a patient's strengths and resources, and preferred to use pragmatism, parsimony, and the least radical intervention in treatment. He believed that the patient is the one who ultimately makes the decision to change or not to change. He strongly encouraged his clients to see themselves as being in the world, rather than define themselves as being in therapy. This change in perspective had to be the continuing focus of Susan's therapy if she was to change her life in a positive way and remove herself from an abusive marriage. The choice was hers, and Doc was doubtful she was going to make that choice.

Susan came to her next appointment on time, was well dressed and groomed and appeared very relaxed. Doc brought her into the office and before he could say anything she said, "I feel in the deep recess of my soul that I am better thanks to you. I don't think I am taking care of Tim anymore and we are very happy. I have decided that I am not going to allow him to abuse me anymore and he said he would stop. Doc, in fact this morning he made me breakfast and brought it to me while I was still in bed. I was so tired after having all of those VIPs from the Pentagon at my house. Tim is the happiest I have ever seen him. His commander called this morning and said he would be getting his promotion by the end of the month. This will be my last appointment and after looking at my watch, I realize that Tim will be expecting me in fifteen minutes to meet him for lunch."

Susan got up and hurried out of the office. As she left, she said, "Doc, if I need you again I will give you a call."

Before Doc could respond, she was inside the elevator door. As Doc ran out to catch her, the doors closed. Doc caught sight of her wiping the tears from her eyes once again. Doc wondered if she would come back or if, in fact, this would be her last appointment.

Susan's willingness to embrace her caretaker role made Doc reflect on the importance of having self-respect, not only for Susan but for all of us. When we allow people to abuse us, as Susan had with Tim, we surrender to fear and lose our self-respect. The only instinct that we tap into in this emotional state is how to survive. Susan was resistant to make any changes because she had become too comfortable in her role as Tim's caretaker. This was the only way Susan could validate her worth and the thought of giving that up was too frightening to her. In her mind, the loss of that role threatened her very survival.

The road toward regaining one's self-respect is a long one, and one that Susan unfortunately was not choosing to take. Doc kept Susan's journal, hoping that maybe one day she will have the courage to open the door, to come back and continue her journey of healing and hope. He hoped that at that time, she wouldn't use superficial changes in Tim's behavior as excuses to slam the door shut. Hopefully one day, Susan will truly find herself and recognize that she is a special person, and that love wasn't about someone abusing her. Abuse is simply about power and control, nothing more and nothing less. Doc promised never to give up on Susan; all she has to do was call for an appointment.

The Buddha remarked, "We travel the whole world with our thoughts, finding nowhere anyone as precious as one's own self. Since each and every person is so precious to themselves, let the self-respecting harm no other being."

No matter where we go, there we are. The ultimate way we escape ourselves is through death; other attempts to do this manifest as what society calls "mental illness" or "emotional disturbance." So many people spend the bulk of their time ignoring themselves, they reach a point that of becoming selfless. Our thoughts and our time become consumed with distractions, which ultimately force us to disengage from the preciousness of this life, and further remove ourselves from the connectedness that we require as members of the human race.

Unfortunately, most of this goes undetected because these mechanisms exist below our consciousness. Although they are seemingly meant to defend us from our fears, the unknown, and anything else that may cause us discomfort, in the long run, they tear at the threads of our existence. People just don't seem willing to embrace their psyche, or face themselves head-on. We are distracted as a people. How do we learn to mind our minds? The challenge facing therapists seems to be to help people rid themselves of the static of distraction (learned behaviors are part of this distraction) and focus on what is most important to them. At the core is the premise that all people want to love, to be loved, and to be respected.

Abuse by one person damages the abused person's very being and psyche. Susan, being unhealthy, was sometimes reluctant to acknowledge and admit that abuse had and was occurring in her marriage. She allowed Tim to manipulate her into this level of docility and thought by constantly pleasing him he would love her. She had been beaten down emotionally, and suffered from low self-esteem that began in her childhood by an absent father and an emotionally detached mother which possibly helped contribute to her feelings of worthlessness, and was convinced that she was incapable of managing her own life without Tim directing it. Susan may have looked at Tim's controlling behaviors as a means of salvation from her lack of assertiveness with regards to her own life.

Tim's behaviors may have reinforced Susan's feelings of worthlessness and her docile attitude may have been attractive to Tim who had control issues, but both of them brought what amounts to the seeds and fertilizer of escalating dysfunction to their relationship. This had similarities to her mother and fathers own relationship.

Tim was an ambitious man who was obviously self-centered, driven and seemed to be totally focused on his career progression. His lack of empathy and seeming belief that his wife was just as anxious for his career to be paramount caused his wife emotional pain. Susan was attracted to Tim because of his ambition and assertiveness, but she was unaware of how selfish his behavior would become in his pursuit of success, and what the cost would be to her. She never envisioned the possible damage Tim's actions would do to the marriage.

The denial that an individual goes through is a skill they employ to cope with their pain. Susan was in denial, but found it too painful to confront the reality of her dysfunctional and codependent relationship with Tim and make the needed changes to become healthier. Susan was carrying a steamer trunk of emotional baggage and either didn't know how to unpack it, or didn't want to unpack it. She got so used to the burden that she normalized it. The fear of losing Tim was greater than the reality of losing her self.

For Susan, abuse was like a narcotic; the first dose from Tim years ago when they were first married knocked her out cold; but then she got accustomed to the numbness every time he abused her.

Doc would tell patients that abuse is like being burned on a hot stove. The first time you get burned you say "Shame on that stove" because you didn't know it would hurt you; the second time you get burned on the same stove you say, "Shame on me," as you obviously haven't learned how to avoid the abuse and protect yourself from it. Therapy teaches skills to use to avoid the hot stove and not get burned by it again.

Doc wondered if Susan would ever come back into therapy, and he began his final clinical assessment and analysis of her case. He knew that in order for Susan to get better, she needed to have the ability to understand and find solutions to her own personal problems. The possible loss of her caretaker role may have scared her so much that it took away her sense of purpose, and she went back to her perception of the moment, and her choice to stay in pain. Susan along with Tim set their emotional baseline years ago in the marriage when Tim emotionally abused her for the first time. Her lack of insight and inability to hold him accountable for his negative and abusive behavior helped to establish the dysfunctional emotional baseline in their marriage. This just reinforced Tim's continued use of this behavior and Susan's acceptance of it.

Susan never came back and Doc knew that her resistance to change and numbness toward Tim's abuse would keep her from moving forward in her healing journey

What a week. Doc was ready for an Aloha weekend.

"Lani, can you turn the lights out and lock up and file Susan Savers case in the file cabinet with all of my other closed cases? I don't think she will be coming back. I am going home for the weekend and spending my time on my favorite beach at north shore near Shark's Cove with Mitzi and the family."

Epilogue

Doc reminisced about his graduate school days, when he learned that the role of the therapist is like the role of a sage. Buddha stated that "A person of wisdom should be truthful, without arrogance, without deceit, not slanderous and not hateful." To this day he tries to live by that wisdom in his personal and professional life. Clients place an enormous amount of trust in their therapists and it is their responsibility to honor that trust. It is a daily task to be reminded of these words of wisdom. When therapists, think they know it all they have become arrogant and can no longer help clients. Over the years Doc has found himself using his skills of discernment and perception to help navigate and guide clients through therapy.

Doc has been formally trained and educated but sometimes he feels that something is missing. In face to face sessions with clients they pour their hearts and souls out to him and sometimes it makes him uncomfortable. Sometimes all they are asking for is feedback or a reframing of their crisis. Doc has found that the most effective therapeutic response is one that is sometimes spontaneous and unrehearsed. Clients have an innate sense that tells them when we are struggling with the information they give to their therapist. They don't realize that they trust their instincts. When the client assesses that the therapist is lost, they lose confidence in the therapist's abilities to help them and the therapeutic alliance is lost. Doc knows that the more he trust his instincts, the less fear he has that something he might say might not be what the client needs to hear. Fear is infectious and others around us can pick up on that emotion, especially clients.

A Christmas Letter From Doc

I want to share a letter I wrote as I also continue to move through my own Personal Journey through Life and my Tales of Change.

No one is exempt from stress and everyone is capable of getting better and living fuller lives everyday we are on the planet if we consciously make the choice to do so.

December 25, 2007

Dear Sis,

Thanks for the CD's and thank your daughter for all of her hard work. I know she took a lot of time and put a lot of love into this project to put these together for the family. The fabric of dysfunction our family had was just a part of what defined our family. Mom and Dad did the best they could do with what they were given to work with as children themselves. As you know there is no book on how to be a parent. I thank God everyday for my parents and all of my family. Mom encouraged me to excel, be tenacious and to be myself. Dad showed me how to relax and have fun in life traveling and not to take life so seriously. Our brother taught me how to be tough and you showed me the path to Meditation which has forever changed my life in so many positive and wonderful ways. I will always be grateful. I focus on the present and I have let the past go a long time ago. My glass is always half full, never half empty. I tell many of my patients that bad stuff hap-

pens to good people and never let the circumstances you find yourself in define who you truly are.

All of my family was very significant in helping me to forge my character into who I am today. I am pleased with my life and what I have accomplished and I know my family would be as well.

I look at the dysfunction we had in our family as necessary for all of us to grow on our spiritual path. If we never have adversity we can never appreciate happiness. Unhappiness is never the situation you are in but your emotions about the situation. All you really need to do is accept this moment fully. You are then in the present and comfortable and content with yourself.

God teaches us to forgive others and ourselves. I have done that in my life. I miss everyday the fun times and memories I have had with my family. From the nights at discos to the poker games and BBQ's at Mom and Dads home, to the werewolves of London moments, to the street fairs on Haight Ashbury to concerts in Golden Gate Park and sunning on Waikiki beach. No one can ever take those happy memories from me.

All of us are on their own personal journey and the family has helped me in their own way help me to define mine.

I think about Mom and Dad often and miss them terribly in my life. I miss the good times with my family but I don't miss all of the nonsense and fights all of us had competing for Mom and Dad's love. We always had their love but they just didn't know how to show it in a healthy way and we didn't know any other way to get their love than by being dysfunctional in our behaviors which produced the constant sibling rivalry that existed between all of us. Acting up in our family was a sure way to get our parent's attention, which is what we all wanted even if it was unhealthy acting up behaviors.

Mom has blessed me with her presence in my home many times since she went to be with God and our father. I know how she so loved these islands and how she blessed my life the last day of hers. I feel blessed by God that I have been allowed to live in such a beautiful and spiritual place and the opportunities to grow spiritually, intellectually, emotionally and to travel the world and see places that I could only dream about as a child in St. Louis and Kansas City. Plus I get Mom visiting me all of the time in Hawaii. Life is good.

I know Mom and Dad are not here physically but I know their love will never die for their children and they will continue to be with each of us on earth as we continue our earthly journey. I know they will be there to greet us when it is our time to go home to be with them and God.

I pray daily that one day soon we can all reunite as a family again and begin a whole new journey that will honor our parents today as evolved and emotionally healthy adults before each of us ends our earthly journey.

May God bless and keep you and your daughters safe always in His loving arms and may God grant you all much Peace and Joy in your lives.

Merry Christmas and Happy New Year to all of you.

God Bless,

Doc

Acknowledgements

1. To my incredible editor and publisher Jean who always kept me focused on the right path with this writing project.

2. To my friend Lieutenant Colonel Leighnor for liking dogs as much as I do and offering me the opportunity of a lifetime to live in Paradise.

3. To Corkie and Gene for their tireless support in listening to my ever changing ideas and helping me to refocus when needed on this project and their constant support.

4. To Mitzipooh who always offers me calm with a wagging tail and calms me with quiet walks, and Lucypooh and Morris whose purring provides me with moments of calm, and to Rotten Cotton.

5. To Jason a good friend who offered me insight and critiqued my work with honesty and wrote a truly gifted and inspired foreword to my book.

6. To my earth parents Marilyn and Herman whose love and support have helped get me through my own rough patches in life.

7. To my friend (U.S. Army Ret Command Sergeant Major) James Euell, who lives and breathes patriotism and is one of the kindest men I have ever had the pleasure of having as a friend and as a mentor.

8. Finally, to God for guiding my hands at the keyboard and helping me select the correct words and for always being my rock.

References

The Teachings of the Buddha. Barnes and Noble Publishing
1993, Jack Kornfield

About the Author

Terry J Martin, LCSW, DCSW is a clinical Social Worker licensed in Hawaii and Missouri. He is currently in private practice in Aiea, Hawaii. He lives with his loving Ohana in Mililani Hawaii. He holds a Masters Degree in Social Work from Washington University, and is currently an adjunct faculty member with the Graduate School of Social Work, University of Hawaii. Terry has also been an adjunct faculty member at the George Warren Brown Graduate School of Social Work, Washington University in St. Louis, Missouri.

He has a specialty treating soldiers and their families dealing with stressors related to deployments, and in treating post traumatic stress disorders and issues related to traumatic brain injury.

He also specializes in conflict management with children, adolescents, and adults. He provides treatment for clients with chemical dependency, domestic violence, marital issues, physical and sexual abuse, conduct disorder, depression, anxiety, and phobias.

He is a professional life coach assisting clients to determine and achieve personal and professional goals by unlocking their full potential.

He is a cognitive behavioral therapist providing individual, family therapy, marriage/couples counseling, and group therapy for adults, children and adolescents. He works with clients to help them view obstacles as opportunities. He believes the patient is the one who ultimately makes the decision to change or not to change.

He emphasizes the patient's strengths and resources. He uses pragmatism, parsimony, and least radical intervention in his clinical practice.

Mr. Martin strongly encourages clients to see themselves as being in the world as more important than in therapy.

Give Us Your E-Pinion!

JMT Publications prides itself on releasing quality products from novice writers with great potential. Our authors would love to hear from you - the reader - and get your feedback on this book. Potential readers benefit from your words as well, and if you help one of them to make a decision, you can get paid for your reviews.

Simply log on to the website, **http://www.epinions.com** and establish an account. Look for *Journeys Through Life* in the Books category. If they don't happen to list it (it takes a while new publications to be listed), start a Reviews page for it! Then, write your heart out. We cherish all good reviews, of course, but we respect your honest opinions.

If you're really enthusiastic, please add your comments and reviews to the *Journeys Through Life* listings at Amazon.com and Alibris.com. Once again, we appreciate your purchase of our product and your opinion.